James Bandinel

Eight Sermons preached before the University of Oxford, in the Year 1780

James Bandinel

Eight Sermons preached before the University of Oxford, in the Year 1780

ISBN/EAN: 9783337159337

Printed in Europe, USA, Canada, Australia, Japan

Cover: Foto ©ninafisch / pixelio.de

More available books at **www.hansebooks.com**

EIGHT SERMONS

PREACHED BEFORE THE

UNIVERSITY of OXFORD,

In the YEAR 1780,

At the LECTURE founded by the late

Rev. and Pious JOHN BAMPTON, M. A.
CANON OF SALISBURY.

TO WHICH IS ADDED,
A VINDICATION OF ST. PAUL
From the Charge of wishing himself accursed,
A SERMON
PREACHED LIKEWISE BEFORE THE UNIVERSITY, ON
SUNDAY, MARCH 14. 1778.

By JAMES BANDINEL, D. D.
OF JESUS COLLEGE, AND PUBLIC ORATOR OF
THE UNIVERSITY.

OXFORD:

Printed for D. Prince and J. Cooke, J. and J. Fletcher;
J. F. and C. Rivington, and T. Cadell, London.
M DCC LXXX.

Imprimatur,

GEO. HORNE,

Mar. 6. 1780.   Vice-Can. Oxon.

TO THE REVEREND

The HEADS of COLLEGES;

THESE SERMONS,

PREACHED

AT THEIR APPOINTMENT,

ARE,

WITH RESPECT

AND AFFECTION,

DEDICATED.

Extract from the last Will and Testament of the late Rev. JOHN BAMPTON, *Canon of* Salisbury.

—— " I give and bequeath my Lands
" and Estates to the Chancellor, Masters,
" and Scholars of the University of Ox-
" ford for ever, to have and to hold all
" and singular the said Lands or Estates
" upon trust, and to the intents and pur-
" poses hereinafter mentioned; that is to
" say, I will and appoint, that the Vice-
" Chancellor of the University of Oxford
" for the time being shall take and re-
" ceive all the rents, issues, and profits
" thereof, and (after all taxes, reparations,
" and necessary deductions made) that he
" pay all the remainder to the endow-
" ment of eight Divinity Lecture Ser-
" mons, to be established for ever in the
" said University, and to be performed in
" the manner following:

" I direct and appoint, that, upon the
" first Tuesday in Easter Term, a Lec-
" turer

"turer be yearly chosen by the Heads of
"Colleges only, and by no others, in the
"room adjoining to the Printing-House,
"between the hours of ten in the morn-
"ing and two in the afternoon, to preach
"eight Divinity Lecture Sermons, the
"year following, at St. Mary's in Ox-
"ford, between the commencement of
"the last month in Lent Term, and the
"end of the third week in Act Term.

"Also I direct and appoint, that the
"eight Divinity Lecture Sermons shall be
"preached upon either of the following
"subjects — to confirm and establish the
"Christian Faith, and to confute all he-
"retics and schismatics—upon the divine
"authority of the Holy Scriptures—upon
"the authority of the writings of the
"primitive Fathers as to the faith and
"practice of the primitive Church —
"upon the Divinity of our Lord and Sa-
"viour Jesus Christ — upon the Divinity
"of the Holy Ghost—upon the Articles
"of the Christian Faith, as comprehend-
"ed in the Apostles' and Nicene Creeds.

"Also

"Also I direct, that thirty copies of the eight Divinity Lecture Sermons shall be always printed, within two months after they are preached, and one copy shall be given to the Chancellor of the University, and one copy to the Head of every College, and one copy to the Mayor of the City of Oxford, and one copy to be put into the Bodleian Library; and the expence of printing them shall be paid out of the revenue of the Lands or Estates given for establishing the Divinity Lecture Sermons; and the Preacher shall not be paid, nor be entitled to the revenue, before they are printed.

"Also I direct and appoint, that no person shall be qualified to preach the Divinity Lecture Sermons, unless he hath taken the Degree of Master of Arts at least, in one of the two Universities of Oxford or Cambridge; and that the same person shall never preach the Divinity Lecture Sermons twice."

The clear income of Mr. Bampton's estate amounts to about 120 *l.* per ann.

CONTENTS.

SERMON I.

PHILIPP. iv. 8.

Whatsoever things are true, whatsoever things are honest, whatsoever things are just, whatsoever things are pure, whatsoever things are lovely, whatsoever things are of good report; if there be any virtue, if there be any praise; think on these things. Page 1

SERMON II.

ROM. x. 14, 15.

How shall they call on him in whom they have not believed? and how shall they believe in him of whom they have not heard? And how shall they hear without a preacher? and how shall they preach, except they be sent? ——— 35

CONTENTS.

SERMON III.

Isaiah lxi. 1, 2.

The Spirit of the Lord is upon me; because the Lord hath anointed me to preach good tidings unto the meek; he hath sent me to bind up the broken-hearted, to proclaim liberty to the captives, and the opening of the prison to them that are bound; to proclaim the acceptable year of the Lord.
                                              79

SERMON IV.

Ephes. i. 3.

Bleſſed be God and the father of our Lord Jeſus Chriſt, who hath bleſſed us with all ſpiritual bleſſings in heavenly places in Chriſt. ——— ——— 119

CONTENTS.

SERMON V.

1 JOHN i. 1, 2, 3.

That which was from the beginning, which we have heard, which we have seen with our eyes, which we have looked upon, and our hands have handled of the word of life (for the life was manifested, and we have seen it, and bear witness, and shew unto you that eternal life which was with the father and was manifested unto us.) That which we have seen and heard declare we unto you. —— —— 157

SERMON VI.

1 COR. xi. 19.

There must be also heresies among you. 197

SERMON VII.

2 PET. i. 19.

We have also a more sure word of prophecy, whereunto ye do well that ye take heed. 231

CONTENTS.

SERMON VIII.

PHIL. iv. 8.

Finally, brethren, whatsoever things are true, whatsoever things are honest, whatsoever things are just, whatsoever things are pure, whatsoever things are lovely, whatsoever things are of good report; if there be any virtue, and if there be any praise, think on these things. —— 267

A Vindication of St. *Paul* from the charge of wishing himself accursed:

A SERMON preached before the University of Oxford.

ROM. ix. 2, 3.

I have great heaviness and continual sorrow in my heart. For I could wish that myself were accursed from Christ for my brethren. 3

SERMON I.

PHILIPP. iv. 8.

Whatsoever things are true, whatsoever things are honest, whatsoever things are just, whatsoever things are pure, whatsoever things are lovely, whatsoever things are of good report; if there be any virtue, if there be any praise; think on these things.

THIS Epistle does not, like many others written by our Apostle, consist of censure and reproof for corrupt doctrines and vicious practices: it abounds on the contrary with expressions and testimonies not only of fervent affection, but likewise chearful confidence. This honourable distinction the *Philippians* certainly had deserved on account of their zeal for St. *Paul* and the part they took in his sufferings, administering to his wants and relieving his necessities: but they had a still higher claim to it by their fortitude in various conflicts with the adversaries of Christ, their constancy in the faith, and stedfastness in the defence and maintenance of the gospel. This he acknowledges with joy and pride; to his commendations for so illustrious an example of fidelity adding nothing but tender and powerful exhortations to preserve their character by the same firm and resolute adherence to the truth, and a generous ambition of excelling in the genuine [a] *fruits of righteousness which are by Jesus Christ unto the glory and praise of God.*

The same testimony of affection and confidence, the same acknowledgement of zeal, commendation for fidelity, and exhortation to a steady continuance in piety and virtue is evidently implied in the preference, by which that worthy person (to fulfill whose pious intentions we are this day assembled) has distinguished those,

[a] *Phil.* i. 11.

whom he has appointed the difpenfers of his munificence for the general improvement of the whole houfehold of God.

This fpiritual relation, which I truft in God holds good between St. *Paul*'s favourite Church and thofe felect members of our own whom I am now addreffing, has naturally led me in my entrance upon this honourable truft to have a more particular attention to this epiftle; of which the paffage I have chofen for my text is the clofe and epilogue; the compendium and fummary of the whole: in which are contained all duties, *fpeculative* and *practical*; *truth*, the foundation; *the moral virtues with their concomitant graces*, the fuperftructure and ornament of the chriftian edifice.

Truth confidered in oppofition to error having its feat in the *fpeculative* is (at leaft in the order of our apprehenfion) antecedent to, and therefore very juftly placed by our Apoftle at, the head of every excellence that can be the object of the *practical* intellect. It is the criterion by which religion is diftinguifhed from mere morality, the caufe and the bafis of genuine virtue and piety; which are the natural, I had almoft faid neceffary, confequence of duly apprehending the nature and the laws of God: and herein the great dignity of truth appears, that it is fo intimately connected with that which forms the perfection and diftinguifhing character of man. Of all the inhabitants of the earth man alone is capable of religion; to worfhip God is his prerogative [b]; and in order to this great and glorious purpofe God created him in his own image, and communicated (if I may fo fpeak) more of himfelf to him than to any other part of this creation, plainly intimating that as without the faculties of reafon and intellect man could not be *capable of religion,* fo without a due exercife of thofe faculties he cannot be truly faid to be *religious*. If this principle is wanting, there can be no folid ground whereon to fix a right practice; all our faireft actions muft lofe their uniformity, beauty, and excellence; the whole

---

[b] Ex tot generibus nullum eft animal præter hominem quod habeat notitiam aliquam Dei. *Cicero de Leg.* l. 1. 18.

fabric

SERMON I.

fabric of religion muſt tumble, being deprived of that ſupport which alone can give it ſtability; becauſe truth being founded on the nature of God muſt be, like its author and original, eternal and immutable [c], *the ſame yeſterday, to-day, and for ever.*

No man yet arrived to that degree of abſurdity in wickedneſs as to deny that it is our duty to act according to our *knowledge*; and ſurely the very ſame reaſon, which makes knowledge the rule of our actions, makes it likewiſe our duty to take all proper methods of acquiring that knowledge, that we may have a ſure and firm foundation whereon to build both our faith and practice. We are indeed told by the church of *Rome*, in excuſe of that ſpiritual tyranny which it has ſet up over the minds of men, that *ignorance is the mother of devotion*; but the fatal experience of many centuries muſt have convinced ſuch even of its own members, as are not totally blinded by prejudice, that it has given birth only to ſuperſtition and infidelity, offsprings well worthy of ſuch a parent.

[c] Heb. xiii. 8.

rent. God has given us reason that we might be influenced by rational motives: without them our belief however true, our worship however pure, cannot properly be called religious; because they want that constitutive principle which, rendering man alone capable of religion, renders him likewise inexcusable if he neglects those communications of himself which God offers him, and obstinately refuses to employ his faculties in the search of spiritual truth, the nature of God, his perfections, and eternal will, the only certain and unerring rule of worship. Ignorance under the means of knowledge, whether careless or presumptuous, so far from being an excuse is an aggravation of guilt: it argues a graceless disposition, abdicates the dignity of human nature, disappoints the purpose which the Almighty aimed at in our creation, despises his honour, and renounces his authority.

Thus in respect of God do both our *duty and gratitude* oblige us to a free and impartial enquiry into the principles upon which religion is built; I say, *free and impartial,*

impartial; for no enquiry can be successful where the reasoning faculties are under any controul from within or without; and it is that very freedom of thinking which makes an intellectual agent responsible for his opinions, as freedom of acting makes a moral one responsible for his actions: the true liberty of both consists in hearkening to the dictates of reason, in a clear unbiassed judgement, and in a power of acting conformably thereunto; and this liberty they both part with, whenever they suffer their will to be directed by any other than its natural and proper motive; which is a right understanding: for then reason is dethroned, their passions govern them even against their judgement, and they become slaves to false appearances, to error, prejudice, and obstinacy.

To suffer such an abuse of our faculties is not only ingratitude and treason against God, but *injustice to ourselves*, a violence done to our nature, whose frame and constitution is admirably adapted to the reception and entertainment of truth. It is often

often by a beautiful and juſt metaphor called the food of the mind; becauſe it nouriſhes and invigorates its faculties, and being homogeneous is eaſily aſſimilated and converted into its very nature and ſubſtance. All other creatures appear to employ their powers upon that which tends to the improvement and perfection of their being. Man feels an active flame within his breaſt which is conſtantly urging him on in the purſuit after knowledge. Can he then juſtify to himſelf the perverſion or even the neglect of this the nobleſt of all principles? ought it not to be employed about the nobleſt object? and what object can be ſo noble as the higheſt and moſt excellent of all beings, his glorious perfections, the different relations we ſtand in to him, and the obligations which ariſe from thoſe relations upon all intelligent beings? The variety and ſublimity of the truths and their real importance and univerſal concernment to the well-being of man all concur to recommend this ſtudy. It is beyond all analogy infinitely ſuperior to every other ſcience: the object is God himſelf, the father of light, the fountain

of

SERMON I.

of all knowledge; and the end of it the glory of God and the happiness of man. This last circumstance adds great weight to the motives already mentioned, and greatly enhances not only the *propriety* but also the *necessity* of our being solicitous and diligent in our endeavours to satisfy ourselves about the evidence, the grounds, and principles of religion.

[d] That there are in the nature of things such principles I take for granted; the notion of a God is universal, and that it was not stamped upon man merely to be the subject of curious and idle speculation, is evident from that natural disposition to worship him which is as universal as the notion. Hence arose the conceit of the Jews, that man was created on the eve of the sabbath, that he might begin his being with the worship of his creator; and even the idolatry of the heathen world clearly owed its rise to this original impression

---

[d] Omnes tamen esse vim & naturam divinam arbitrantur. Nec verò id collocutio hominum aut consensus efficit; non institutis opinio est confirmata, non legibus. Omni autem in re consensio omnium gentium lex naturæ putanda est. *Cicer. Tusc. quæst.* l. 1. c. 13.

however

however perverted, to a conviction however misapplied, of this natural duty. They could not totally raze out, but they defaced and disfigured the characters of God written upon the soul; they did not deny his being, but worshipped the creature [e] παρὰ τὸν κτίσαντα *beside* or *in conjunction with* the creator. This subject has been so copiously handled, and the being and providence of God so fully and undeniably proved by many learned and pious men, that I hold it altogether needless to enter into a tedious repetition, or attempt a new arrangement of their arguments. Why should I dwell, especially before this audience, on the harmony, preservation, and symmetry of the whole universe, the wonderful fabrick of our bodies, and the still more wonderful faculties of our souls, when our imperfections themselves lead us by an easy and plain inference to an irrefragable proof of our dependance upon a superior being? for as the idea of self-existence necessarily excludes all imperfections, whatever is imperfect must have some higher cause, which insensibly leads us to the au-

[e] *Rom.* i. 25.

thor

thor of all beings, who has no cause without himself. As I have therefore hitherto argued, so shall I continue to argue, without a formal discussion of what I think ought to be assumed as an axiom in philosophy; not only because to require a proof of that, of which our very being is a demonstration, implies something not unlike an absurdity; but likewise because revelation, which is to be the subject of these discourses, necessarily includes within it the idea of a God to grant that revelation; the truth of which being proved, by the same arguments will of course be proved the existence and divinity of its author.

As the idea of a God is included in that of a revelation, so will I not scruple to affirm that a divine revelation is a necessary consequence of the existence of God. It seems (with reverence be it spoken) altogether inconsistent with either the wisdom or goodness of God to have made moral agents without prescribing them some law, to require worship and services without some declaration or information, however conveyed, of the worship and services which
would

would be accepted; for thefe the nobleft and moſt uſeful parts of knowledge, and confequently the moſt neceſſary and fit to be learned, as they are ſtiled by Plato, *ᶠ no man* (adds the fame philoſopher) *can teach except he be firſt taught of God*. If therefore unaſſiſted reaſon is unequal to this taſk (and the authority of ſo great a maſter of reaſon is ſurely in this caſe concluſive) it is more than probable that God did not leave our firſt parent, in a ſtate of darkneſs and uncertainty, expoſed to all the miſeries which ſpring from ignorance and error; but originally gave him ſome rule of life, diſcovered to him by immediate revelation all the neceſſary truths of what is called natural religion. If theſe truths and the duties reſulting from them came in proceſs of time by whatever accident to be forgotten, the expediency of a ſupernatural information recurs; for as in *corporeal*, ſo likewiſe in *ſpiritual* blindneſs, when the faculty of ſight is entirely loſt, no power

---

ᶠ Ἀλλ᾽ ὀδ᾽ ἂν διδάξειεν ἢ μὴ Θεὸς ὑφηγοῖτο. *Epinom.* There are many paſſages of the fame import interſperſed in all his works; particularly *in the fourth book de Rep. Apol. Socrat.* and the *Phædo*.

ſhort

short of omnipotence is equal to the renewal of it: it is a new creation; for from total privation to absolute restoration, the distance is the same as from non-entity to existence: and, whenever God pleases to interpose, the same obedience which was due to the first, is due likewise to every subsequent declaration of his will, the validity of each being derived from the same authority. Whoever therefore believes in God, being under a natural obligation of conforming to his will when known, is necessarily bound to enquire whether he has given any particular revelation of it, and consequently, when there are pretensions to it, to examine seriously and impartially the evidences upon which such pretensions are grounded. The necessity of some information more than human we have seen acknowledged by Plato, and many other passages to the same purpose might have been adduced out of his writings, as well as those of his great *Roman* interpreter. The account indeed, which the latter gives us of the absurdity and impiety of both the *philosophical* and *religious* tenets of his time, renders it highly

highly probable upon principles of mere reason that God, whose mercy is over all his works, would interfere in behalf of his creatures, restore primitive truth, and rescue religion from superstition and idolatry.

That the divine interposition is not contrary to our natural notions is evident from a common opinion, which prevailed in all ages and countries, that their founders and legislators had conferences with, and received instructions from, some superior being; whose authority they pleaded for both their political and religious institutions. These testimonies unbelievers, those at least who assume to themselves the venerable name of philosophers, would do well to consider before they dismiss Christianity in their usual disingenuous manner, without examining into its pretensions, nay without even giving it a hearing, upon the bare supposition that a revelation from God is at best incredible if not impossible. Its pretensions surely entitle it to more civility and respect.

Without

SERMON I.

ᵉ Without controverſy great is the myſtery of godlineſs; great are the bleſſings which it promiſes, great the knowledge which it profeſſes to teach, the knowledge of **God** and of ourſelves, the eternal principles of truth, the duties reſulting from thoſe principles, and the proper motives and encouragements to enforce thoſe duties. It tenders to loſt mankind, who lay under the breach and yet under the bond of the covenant of works, terms of reconciliation, pardon, and peace: God's law was broken, his will diſobeyed, his name diſhonoured; and yet he propitiates, he expiates our ſins againſt himſelf, he receives us into favour again, he grants us his word to direct and his grace to aſſiſt us in the performance of our duty, which performance he promiſes to reward with eternal happineſs in a better world. Doctrines theſe of no mean and trivial importance, of no inferior and ſubordinate kind; to which Chriſtianity moreover demands our attention for the ſake, and under the authority, of the everlaſting God who dictated and his eternal ſon who publiſhed them.

ᵉ 1 *Tim.* iii. 16.

Under

Under such sanction no wonder that it assumes the emphatical name of *truth*; that it is stiled by way of eminence [h] *the word of truth,* [i] *the truth of God*; that the belief and the knowledge of it are called [k] *the belief and the* [l] *knowledge of the truth*; that they who profess it are said [m] *to be of the truth,* and they that reject it [n] *not to believe,* [o] *not to obey the truth.* Claims of so high a nature and of so great importance to man, made so seriously, deserve surely to be seriously considered and carefully examined; lest haply, through our wilful neglect and indifference, we be found to slight God's gifts, suspect his goodness, call his truth and of course all his essential perfections into question; for whosoever despises a law casts dishonour upon the authority that enjoins it.

How justly *Christianity* appropriates to itself the title of truth cannot but appear to every unprejudiced mind that considers

[h] *Ephes.* i. 3, &c.   [i] *Rom.* iii. 7, &c.   [k] 2 *Thessal.* ii. 13.
[l] 1 *Tim.* ii. 4, &c.   [m] 1 *John* iii. 19.   [n] 2 *Thess.* ii. 12.
[o] *Rom.* ii. 8.

it

SERMON I.

it in opposition to both the falshood of *paganism* and to the promises and shadows of *judaism*. With regard to the *pagan religion* (if an ill-contrived texture of inconsistent impostures can be called by so sacred a name) little pains need be taken to shew the vanity and the folly of it, since even [p] from among those who professed it there are not wanting men, and those of superior knowledge and understanding, who testify their dislike and contempt of those ridiculous and beastly fables upon which their theology and worship depended. They dissembled indeed and outwardly complied out of policy and fear; or, if a higher motive may be assigned for their compliance [q], it was by no means (as they themselves acknowledged) an opinion that it was acceptable to the

---

[p] Hæc et dicuntur et creduntur stultissimè, et plena sunt futilitatis summæque levitatis. *Cicer. de nat. Deor.* l. 2.

[q] Quæ omnia sapiens servabit tanquam legibus jussa non tanquam diis grata. *Seneca apud August. de civit. Dei.* l. 6. 10.

Retinetur autem et ad opinionem vulgi et ad magnas utilitates reipublicæ mos, religio, disciplina, jus augurum, collegii auctoritas. *Cicer. de divin.* l. 2. Διί φυλάσσειν τα τις κοινὸν κεκυρωμένα· — παρελύειν ἐχ ὅσιον τὰ ἐξ ἀρχῆς κ᾽ τόπες νενομισμένα. *Cels. apud Orig.* l. 5.

B   deity,

deity, but only political intereſt and a reſpect which they thought due to the laws and cuſtoms of their country. It ſeems indeed of all paradoxes the leaſt reconcileable to the human mind, how man not totally diveſted of reaſon could believe in and pay adoration to ſuch a ridiculous and contemptible rabble of deities, terreſtrial and infernal as well as celeſtial, male and female, guilty of fornication, adultery, inceſt, and every unnatural luſt; thieves, drunkards, murderers, parricides : nay ſome worſhipped even brute beaſts of the the loweſt and vileſt kind, things without life, without being; the produce of their gardens, the diſeaſes of their bodies, the paſſions and vices of their minds. Theſe they numbered among things venerable and divine; to theſe they dedicated temples, and offered ſacrifices with ſuch ſuperſtitious devotion, ſuch filthy and inhuman rites, as were ſuitable to the objects of their worſhip. From ſuch unſeemly notions what glory to God or benefit to man could accrue? Such opinions and practices reſpecting religion (one of the firſt principles of which is to imitate the deity)

SERMON I. 19

deity) muft neceffarily produce fimilar opinions and practices with regard to morality: and that this was really the cafe, is abundantly evinced by their own writers, fuch in particular as lived about the beginning of Chriftianity; whofe accounts of the horrid depravation of manners bear ample teftimony to that fhocking catalogue of abominable vices, with which the gentiles are charged by St. *Paul* in the beginning of his epiftle to the *Romans*. Some indeed of the philofophers were not entirely ignorant of the leading principles of natural religion; yet what did all their ftudies, all their enquiries and difputations produce except uncertainty, diffatisfaction, and perplexity; inftead of full conviction, fome faint conjecture; in the room of folid perfuafion, unfteady and irreconcileable variety of opinion? *Varro* who was called the wifeft of the Romans, reckons up (as he is quoted by ' St. *Auftin*) two hundred and eighty eight different fentiments concerning happinefs, and ⁹ *Themiftius* tells the emperor *Valens*, that there

---
' *De civit. Dei.* l. 1. 19. 1.   ⁹ *Sozomen.* l. 6. 36.

were

were above three hundred jarring opinions among the philosophers of Greece; no wonder therefore that ' *Maximus Tyrius* acknowledges himself at a loss which of the schools to follow, under which of the innumerable sects of philosophers to enlist. Being scholars of nature only, their knowledge could reach no farther than what nature taught: so far therefore were they from having a perfect rule of life, an entire system of either divinity or morality, that " ᵘ about these things neither nation " agreed with nation, nor city with city, "· nor family with family, nor one man " with another, nor any one with him-" self."

What a different scene does the *gospel of Christ* exhibit! God has impressed upon it signatures of himself, characters that plainly evince its divine origin. The *speculative* part represents God to us as a being absolutely free from all imperfec-

---

ᵗ *Dissert.* 19. *Edit. Oxon.* which concludes with these remarkable words ὁρᾷς τὸ πλῆθ‍ῶ τ῀ ἡγεμόνων· ὁρᾷς τὸ πλῆθ‍ῶ τ῀ συνθημάτων· πῆ τις τράπηται; ποῖον αὐτῶν καταδέξωμαι; τίνι πεισθῶ τ῀ παραγγελμάτων;

ᵘ *Id. Dissert.* 1.

tions

tions and possessed of all perfections whatsoever in the highest degree; it ascribes to him every thing that is great and glorious, good and amiable. The worship it enjoins is suitable to the idea of so excellent and pure a deity: it consists of an awful sense of his majesty and our dependence upon him, love of his perfections, faith in his veracity, gratitude for his benefits, recourse to his goodness, frequent meditations upon him, communion with him and an inward desire to please him. These things are required to be performed by us with fervency and zeal, with reverence, humility, and sincerity.—*" God is a spirit, and they that worship him must worship him in spirit and in truth.* With this superior excellence of the speculative part of our religion the *practical* entirely agrees. It is not, like the morality taught in the schools of the heathen, made up of shreds and patches, modelled according to the different genius and interest of different states and ages, furnishing in one century perhaps one truth and in another century

" *John* iv. 24.

another

another truth: It is one simple, uniform, and perfect rule of life; built upon the most solid foundation, the authority of God and our obedience to his will; it is suited to all times and all places, productive of the universal good of every human society. The laws which it enjoins proceed not from mere power and authority, but are evidently acts of wisdom and goodness. There is no precept delivered, no duty recommended, but what is highly rational and useful, worthy of God and beneficial to man; from the observance of them will naturally result peace and tranquillity of mind, good will from all men, and the favour and acceptance of God; who to our sincere though imperfect obedience has been moreover graciously pleased to annex the glorious promise of *joys, such [x] as eye has not seen, ear heard, neither hath it entered into the heart of man to conceive*. These doctrines are peculiar to Christianity; philosophy never taught them in her schools, neither are they to be read in the book of nature; for, after

[x] 1 *Cor.* ii. 9.

all the glorious things which are spoken of reason, it never furnished mankind with more than a bare surmise of futurity, a feeble hope of that *ʸ most desirable thing which* Seneca observes *their great men promised, but could not prove:* It is revelation alone that can improve conjecture into knowledge, and doubt into certainty.

Thus does the *gospel of Christ* in opposition to *paganism* claim the title of *truth* on account of the intrinsic excellence and sublimity of its doctrines. It moreover challenges it with respect to the *jewish religion*; it is the body of its shadows, the substance of its figures, the completion of its promises. And here a new scene opens, a comprehensive view of a vast, uniform, and consistent plan; which could not be carried on under different dispensations for such a length of time, with the utmost analogy and harmony, by any thing less than the fore-knowledge and providence of God. Every part of the mosaical

---

ʸ Credebam opinionibus magnorum virorum rem gratissimam promittentium magis quam probantium. *Senec. Ep.* 102. See *Whitby* upon 2 *Tim.* i. 10.

SERMON I.

oeconomy was typical of that more perfect one, which was to be established when [z]*the Lord would make a new covenant with the house of Israel,* when [a] *the figures for the time then present,* [b] *the shadows of things to come,* were to have their accomplishment in Christ, the true ark [c] *in whom dwelleth all the fulness of the godhead bodily,* as it did symbolically in the tabernacle and afterwards in the temple; the true mercy-seat [d], *through which God shews himself gracious to his people;* the true paschal lamb [e], *whose blood protects us from the destroying angel;* the true piacular victim [f], *whom God hath set forth to be a propitiation for the remission of sins;* the true high priest [g], *who having obtained an eternal redemption, is not entered into the holy places made with hands which are the figures of the true, but into heaven itself now to appear in the presence of God for us.* These are but few out of the numberless typical analogies which might be produced; yet sufficient, I trust, to shew that the foundations of the gospel were

---

[z] *Jer.* 31. 31.   [a] *Heb.* viii. 9.   [b] *Coloss.* ii. 17.
[c] *Coloss.* ii. 9.   [d] *Exod.* 20, &c.   [e] *Exod.* 12.
[f] *Rom.* iii. 25.   [g] *Heb.* ix. 12, 24.

laid

laid in the law. [h] Every part of the *ritual* worship bore an emblematical relation to the *spiritual* one which was to succeed it; every external dispensation of Providence to the Jews had a mystical respect to the everlasting covenant with all nations, and the whole people was figurative of the spiritual *Israel* or the church of the *Messiah*, who was shadowed forth to them under types and ceremonies; the amazing correspondency of which with that dispensation, which they prefigured so many ages before its appearance, clearly demonstrates them to have been the effect not of chance but of wisdom power and foresight, and fully ratifies and confirms the veracity of God [i] *whose promises in Christ are yea and amen.*

Here let us pause awhile to admire how God is pleased to accommodate the operations of his grace to the course of nature. Nothing arrives to its full age and maturity but by gentle successive degrees. Even man himself, the Lord of the creation, comes

---

[h] See *Berriman's Sermons at Boyle's Lecture.*
[i] 2 Cor. i. 20.

on flowly to his perfection through the imbecillity of childhood and the defects of youth. Analogous to this order of things he brought us to the day-light of the gospel through the dark night of paganism and the twilight of the law. When he took his church from under the hand of nature, he trained and tutored it in elements fitted for a weak capacity; elements of a sensible and material nature, yet so admirably contrived as to be emblematical of that true spiritual doctrine, the splendor of which being too strong for its infancy was veiled at first under the cloud of the mosaical administration, but in fulness of time brought to light by the gospel.

[k] It is an objection as old as the time of *Celsus* (which, however false and repeatedly shewn to be such, has yet never failed to be urged with great confidence by all his successors in infidelity) that Christianity debars its professors from all enquiries about religious truths, and demands of them a full and implicit assent without a previous

---

[k] Μὴ ἐξέταζε ἀλλὰ πίστευσον. *Origen.* L. 1.

exami-

examination of the ground on which they are to build that affent. But furely never was objection raifed upon fo flight a foundation. Chriftianity with a candour peculiar to itfelf earneftly folicits a trial at the bar of reafon, invites and exhorts every man, before he embraces its doctrines, fairly and impartially to examine its pretenfions.[l] *Prove all things*, fays St. *Paul, hold faft that which is good.* When St. *John* warns us againft believing every fpirit, and bids us [m] *try the fpirits whether they are of God*, does he not plainly recommend the ufe of our own underftanding againft a blind implicit belief? Is not the fame advice fairly implied in the commendation given to the *Bereans* for [n] *fearching the fcriptures* and enquiring into the truth of what the apoftles preached? And does not our Saviour himfelf inculcate the fame doctrine when he appeals to the judgement of his adverfaries, [o] *Why do ye not even of yourfelves judge what is right?*

Falfhood indeed and error delight in darknefs; there is fomething in them fo

[l] *Theff.* v. 21.   [m] 1 *Ep.* iv. 1.   [n] *Acts* xvii. 11.
Luke xii. 57.

disguftful

disgustful and contemptible that they must keep at a distance, out of sight, if they mean to acquire love or reverence. Hence the mysteries of the heathen were surrounded on all sides by a thick impenetrable veil: they were practiced in the night; none were admitted to them but under a solemn and dreadful oath of secrecy; whoever disclosed any part of them was excluded from all the rights and benefits of civil society, he was apprehended as a public offender and suffered death. On the contrary nothing dishonours *truth* so much as concealment; the more it is seen the more awful and lovely it appears; *its tabernacle is placed in the sun*, it never looks so glorious as when it shines in full meridian splendor. While therefore the founders and dispensers of fabulous religions and absurd worship cover them under silence and obscurity, the Gospel in strict conformity to its character professedly reveals mysteries; *Christ*, so far from enjoining secrecy to his apostles, exhorts them to a free profession and open publication of his doctrines. ᵖ *What*

ᵖ *Matt.* x. 27.

I say

SERMON I.

I say to you in darkness, speak ye in the light; i. e. the doctrines which I teach you in parables do ye publicly explain and expound. *What ye hear in the ear, that preach ye upon the house-tops;* i. e. what I more privately impart to you, do ye courageously publish and proclaim to all the world. This fair and candid proceeding ought, one would imagine, to procure at least a favourable hearing; and how little Christianity declines, nay how truly it affects and courts, the verdict of unbiassed reason might justly be collected (were the more direct proofs we have just urged wanting) from its making its appearance in the brightest day of human knowledge. Had it been conscious of its own weakness, it would not thus boldly have entered the lists against the prejudices of mankind, when the great improvement and increase of all kinds of literature had excited a noble spirit of curiosity, which not only prompted men to enquire after, but qualified them to understand and examine truth and detect fraud and imposture. But in this as well as other respects [q] *wisdom has*

[q] *Matth.* xi. 19.

been

been justified of her children. [r] When the books written by *Numa* the father of the Roman religion, and by him ordered to be buried under ground, were accidentally found four hundred years after; his motives for the religious establishment, which he imposed upon the credulity of a rude illiterate nation, appeared to a more enlightened age so trivial and frivolous, that they were burned by a public decree of the senate: The *imposture of Mahomet* as well as the *pagan idolatry* arose in times of general corruption ignorance, and barbarism; but *Christianity*, the system of that worship which comes recommended with the character of truth, has constantly kept pace with knowledge; it appeared when the sciences were arrived at their highest perfection, grew by the aids of learning, has decayed and revived with it; it has constantly appealed to reason, and from every trial upon that test has as constantly acquired fresh strength, credit, and authority.

This confidence, as has been observed, is peculiar to Christianity, and perfectly agree-

[r] *Varro apud August. de civit. Dei* vii. 24.

able

able to the character of *truth*; which, like its symbol in the material world, chearfully spreading its rays over the whole universe is hid from none but those who wilfully shut their eyes against it. But, lest too great a torrent of light immediately succeeding thick darkness might oppress the intellectual sight, the wisdom and the goodness of God previously prepared mankind for that gracious dispensation which he intended them, and made the knowledge of the *law* the forerunner of the knowledge of the *gospel* even among the gentiles.' The books of the *old* testament, in which the *new* is virtually involved, being (not without the conduct of providence) translated some ages before into Greek the then general language, the treasures of the *jewish* and consequently the *christian* religion were laid open to other nations as well as the Jews, and gradually disposed them the more readily to receive that great prophet and saviour of mankind; who had been so often and so plainly foretold in prophecies, which they themselves knew to have been

' See *universal history* V. 10. p. 244.

written

written many centuries before their completion.

And now let the infidel (who exclaims againſt chriſtianity as requiring a groundleſs faith and obtruding itſelf upon men in the dark) ſearch the records of antiquity and diſcover, if he can, another religion that contains doctrines equally worthy of God, precepts equally conducive to the good of man; a religion, that confiding in the merits of its cauſe invites men to make uſe of their beſt underſtanding; a religion, that appeals to the principles of another religion then in being in all appearance totally different from itſelf; yet when ſurveyed together with it forming a beautiful, regular, and compleat ſyſtem, carried on through ſucceſſive ages and periods with an analogy ſurpriſingly harmonious and uniform: a religion moreover, that, to remove all ſuſpicion of impoſture, communicates the knowledge of the law on which it is founded ſome hundred years before its appearance, and at laſt fully diſcovers itſelf at a time when the intellectual improvements of mankind enable them thoroughly

to

to examine and judge of the truth of its pretenfions.

Till this is done (and that it cannot be done we may fairly infer from its having never been attempted) we cannot forego the exclufive claim which Chriftianity has to the facred name of *truth*, and of courfe to our ferious, diligent, and impartial attention, even upon thefe prefumptive proofs of its proceeding from God.

That it did really proceed from God we have, I truft, good and fufficient evidence; and this with his affiftance fhall be the fubject of the following difcourfe.

SERMON II.

Rom. x. 14, 15.

How shall they call on him in whom they have not believed? and how shall they believe in him of whom they have not heard? And how shall they hear without a preacher? and how shall they preach, except they be sent?

ALTHOUGH the arguments produced in the preceding discourse might to some appear fully sufficient to justify the claim which the gospel makes to the title of truth; yet as that kind of reasoning, which arises from the nature and intrinsic excellence of a doctrine, is by

others

others looked upon as inconclusive; I think it not improper (in order to obviate all objections) to enquire into some at least of the *external* evidence, by which this *internal* one is supported. And in truth, after all that has been said in favour of each of these methods, they seem to me to stand mutually in need of each other's assistance. A revelation opposite to the principles of nature and the reason of things is a contradiction in terms; and therefore no external evidence whatsoever can establish the divinity of a religion, which carries within it such unquestionable proofs of a different origin; neither are the interior marks of truth, though necessary and inseparable characters, absolute and infallible proofs of an immediate revelation. But when both conspire together; when to the testimony, which a religion itself bears to its own authority, is added every external one which circumstances require, supported by such proofs as the nature of the thing will admit, nothing but obstinacy can withold its assent, scepticism becomes folly, incredulity a sin.

As

SERMON II.

As therefore not only the principles and doctrines of the Christian divinity, but likewise the external proofs by which they are confirmed, are contained in the books of the *old* and *new testament*; I flatter myself I cannot better engage your attention, or more faithfully discharge the trust reposed in me, than by first establishing the truth and authority of the scriptures; because upon them the truth and authority of our holy religion ultimately depend: for the authenticity of the history being acknowledged, and the facts which are therein recorded being granted, the testimony of *miracles* and *prophecies* joined to the *excellence of the doctrines* is a clear and compleat demonstration of our Saviour's divine commission; by them God attests the whole oeconomy of grace to be an immediate revelation from heaven as certainly as that he cannot lie or give his approbation to a lie.

Before I enter upon particular proofs, I beg leave to remind you that*, as the idea

* See *page* 11.

of a God constantly carries with it the idea of some service or worship due to him, so does it (according to my apprehensions) necessarily suppose a revelation, a declaration from God of what service and worship will be acceptable to him. Knowledge must in the course of things ever precede obedience; and therefore in every well-regulated state the law is always promulged before the observance of it is required. The will of God is the only law for our belief and practice; for who is to prescribe where God is concerned, except God himself? But [b] *who hath known the mind of the Lord, or who hath been his counsellor?* How shall we attain at the knowledge of his will, except from himself and those to whom he has been pleased to reveal it? From this argument St. *Paul* in my text infers the necessity of his mission to preach the gospel among the gentiles: it holds good in all cases, and is a strong presumption in favour of the scriptures; for supposing a revelation necessary, where else are we to look for it?

[b] *Rom.* xi. 34.

Where

SERMON II.

Where shall we find, I will not say a *better* but, *another* declaration of the will of God except in those volumes which we receive as the word of God ? Is not therefore the conduct of a wilful obstinate infidel nearly similar to that of a mariner; who in a dark tempestuous night, without either compass or pilot, should perversely prefer the perils of an unknown sea to the security of the only port that offers itself.

But from this *general* argument let us descend to *particulars*; premising first, that there is such a connexion and relation between the two testaments, that the same proofs illustrate and confirm both; the *new* testament is founded on the *old*, the *old* accomplished in the *new*; the truth of the one being allowed, the truth of the other follows of course.

The first evidence I shall produce in favour of the scriptures is their *antiquity*. Of this argument the first apologists for Christianity make frequent use against their pagan adversaries; and with great propriety, for amongst them the most ancient acts were reckoned the moſt authentic. *ᶜApud vos quoque* (ſays Tertullian) *religionis eſt inſtar fidem de temporibus aſſerere.* We can (ſays ᵈ Cicero) *ſupport this opinion,* the immortality of the ſoul, *by the authority of the beſt writers, which in all caſes ought to have and has great weight, but principally by that of all antiquity; which, the nearer it approached to the origin of things and the divine offspring, the better probably did it diſcern the truth.* In this, as in almoſt every part of his philoſophy, he copies from his grecian maſter the *atticizing Moſes,* as ᵉ *Numenius* ſtiles *Plato;* who in his *Philebus* ſpeaking, as many learned interpreters think, of an unity and plurality in the godhead makes uſe of the ſame authority; *the ancients, ſays he, who were better than us, and dwelt nearer to the*

ᶜ *Apol.* c. 9.

ᵈ Auctoribus ad iſtam ſententiam—uti optimis poſſumus —et primum quidem omni *antiquitate:* quæ quo propius aberat ab ortu et divinâ prôgenie hoc melius ea fortaſſe quæ erant vera cernebat. *Tuſc. Quæſt.* 1. 12. *Plato* in his *Timæus* calls the firſt men *the offspring and the children of the Gods.*

ᵉ Νυμήνιθ- δὲ ὁ Πυθαγόρειος φιλόσοφθ- ἄντικρυς γράφει, τί γάρ ἐςι Πλάτων ἢ Μωσῆς ἀτΊικίζων; *Clem. Alex. Strom.* l. 1. Vide *Suid.* in voce Νυμήνιθ-.

Gods,

SERMON II.

Gods, have tranſmitted down this tradition. The force of this reaſoning is tacitly acknowledged by that univerſal conſent, with which all mankind ſeem to conſpire in paying reſpect and reverence to antiquity. And to this inartificial argument, reaſon readily ſuſcribes; for truth is the eldeſt born of heaven, evidently and of neceſſity prior to falſhood; becauſe falſhood is nothing elſe but a corruption of the truth: and therefore ᶠ among the characters and criteria of heavenly writings antiquity deſervedly has its place; for from thence they acquire much dignity and authority above all human books and records, ᵍ which (as has been fully proved by a learned writer of our own) borrowed all their choiceſt notions and contemplations as well natural and moral as divine from the ſacred oracles, in that reſpect bearing teſtimony to the truth of them; and, where they differ, it is but juſt to give credit to the elder who drew their doctrines from the fountain-head.

ᶠ *Bochart's Phaleg.*
ᵍ See *Gale's Court of the gentiles.*

I ſhall

SERMON II.

I shall not pay so bad a compliment to this audience as to attempt a laboured proof of the antiquity of *Moses:* he was in fact prior to most of the fabulous deities; and having in his youth conversed with men who were cotemporaries with *Joseph,* perhaps with *Jacob,* might have had those facts, which he was not an eye witness of himself, transmitted by a regular chain of traditions connected but by very few links with the inhabitants of the antediluvian world. The matter of his history, and the manner in which it is recorded, suit entirely with this antiquity. There is no account in any other writer of the creation or the fall of man; something indeed like the fall is here and there obscurely hinted; but *Moses* alone gives us the history and the cause of it. He alone teaches us the age of the world, the origin and dispersion of mankind, the beginning and succession of kingdoms. This account is embellished with no shew of learning; it is written with a majestic security, short and plain; as we may well suppose the first memoirs to have been, whilst

SERMON II. 43

whilst religion was wisdom, simple truth philosophy; and therefore [h] *Tatian*, a man well versed in all kinds of human literature, ingenuously acknowledges that one of the chief reasons of his embracing the christian religion was the rational account he there met with of the creation of all things. *Varro* confesses the first period of profane history to be entirely unknown, and the second fabulous; those therefore among the heathens, who treat of primitive antiquity, conceal their ignorance under the specious veil of mystical allegories; and so effectually envelop themselves within an infinite multitude of incoherent generations, that it is impossible for the most sagacious interpreter to trace either their history or philosophy. But with *Moses* there is nothing unknown or fabulous; he is every where clear and consistent, particularly specifies every minute circumstance as well known and fresh in his memory, and connects all the remarkable periods but by a very few links; which on account of the long lives of the

[h] *Orat. contra Græc.* c. 46.

patriarchs

patriarchs touch each other, and made it very eafy for his cotemporaries to have detected him, if in facts fo recent and fo arranged he had been guilty of any falfhood. Even in thofe books which were written after the Hebrew volumes had been tranflated into Greek, and which treat of the *Egyptian, Chaldean,* and *Phœnician* antiquities, you have nothing but a heap of undigefted fables and confufed traditions for fome ages fubfequent to *Mofes* himfelf; and yet the motive of their authors evidently was to prove, in contradiction to *Mofes*, that the Jews were by no means fuperior in point of age or origin to their refpective nations; a plain proof of the refpect which men in general have for antiquity, and how ftrongly they connect it with the idea of dignity and reverence.

The argument from *antiquity* acquires a very confiderable degree of ftrength, when joined to that of *a perpetual and uninterrupted tradition*. To have been in quiet poffeffion fo long is no mean prefumptive proof in favour of the poffeffor. The authenticity and authority of the *old teftament* has been

SERMON II. 45

been allowed by the *Christians* for near two thousand years; and if we ascend higher we shall find the *Jews* universally and without any chasm acknowledging it for above fourteen hundred years more. Now two people, entirely differing in other respects, could not possibly have entered into a combination; the appeal therefore, which they both make to *Moses* and the *prophets*, not only presupposes but is a confirmation of their unquestioned veracity. [i] When the descendants of *Jacob* left *Egypt*, the men exclusive of the women and children amounted to above *six hundred thousand*: they were all witnesses of the facts recorded in four of the books written by *Moses*: Is it credible, is it possible, that so many persons could, against the testimony of their senses, believe the account of numberless miracles said to have been performed, and in consequence of that belief submit to a rigorous and painful law, every part of which was impressed with characters of severity and servitude? Their ceremonies and solemn fes-

[i] *Exod.* xii. 37. *Numb.* i. 46.

tivals,

tivals, though typically looking forwards to their *spiritual* accomplishment yet, had a retrospect to former *temporal* deliverances; and having been instituted in memory of them, bore a constant and unbiassed testimony to the truth of the historian. These were strictly enjoined under heavy penalties; and [k] at several of them all the males were obliged to leave their affairs, their homes, and families, and appear from every part of the kingdom before the Lord at *Jerusalem*. Would a people, famous for obstinacy and rebellion, have submitted for so long a time as they did to the bondage of a law, the observance of which was attended with so much inconvenience, if they had not been thoroughly convinced of the reality of those transactions which the festivals were appointed to commemorate?

From the time of *Moses* downwards the history is (if possible) still carried on with greater precision and accuracy through the

---

[k] At the three grand festivals, the *passover*, the *feast of the weeks*, and the *feast of the tabernacle*. *Deuter.* xvi. 16, &c.

several

several successions of *judges* and *kings*, the length of their respective governments ascertained, and the chronology every where settled till the *Babylonish* captivity; their deliverance from which, and re-settlement in *Judea*, are particularly described by *Ezra*, an eye witness of every circumstance, a writer of an unimpeached character; and, though the last in the *Jewish* canon, cotemporary with *Herodotus* the father of *Grecian* history: a remarkable circumstance, which fixes beyond all dispute the right which the acts and monuments of the *old testament* have to superior antiquity; and, when joined with another still more remarkable circumstance, may justify a conjecture that it was not without the appointment of providence, that in *historical* as well as *religious* truths all nations lighted their candle at the fire of the sanctuary. For surely it was owing to somewhat more than chance, that certainty should disdain to dwell in other lands till it had been banished from *Judea*, that all the famous epochs of other people though entirely unconnected (such as the *æra of Nabonassar, the olympiads of Greece,*

Greece, and the *foundation of Rome*) should all begin at the same time; and that time be the period marked out for the destruction of the jewish nation; when God was pleased to raise up two mighty empires to be his instruments for the punishment of his own people, and the overthrow of the kingdoms of *Israel* and *Judah*.

But to return.—We have the same *universal and uninterrupted tradition* for the authenticity of the *new testament*; and if the validity of this evidence is called in question there is an end of public faith, human converse must subsist without human confidence. We have received these sacred volumes from our forefathers, they from theirs, and so on backwards in a continued series up to those who lived in the time of the *Apostles*, who heard them deliver the same doctrines, and knew for certain that they published them in those writings which go under their names. They are universally quoted by all the fathers without intermission, and by them assigned to those authors whose names they now

now bear. And what other authority, than the evidence of those who were cotemporary with or lived near the times of the writer, and the perpetual consent of learned men, can we have for assigning particular books to particular authors? But in this the scriptures have a very singular advantage over every other composition whatsoever; they can alledge for their genuineness what no other volumes have the least pretension to, *a judicial sanction*: they have been approved and confirmed by men of the greatest learning in different ages, solemnly assembled in more than a thousand *provincial*, and not less than twenty *general* councils.

Add to this the confirmation which they receive from *the testimony of heretics*; the writings of *Moses* from the *Samaritans* irreconcileable separatists from the *Jews*: and the books of the *new testament* from *sectaries* of all ages and denominations, who have always pretended the authority of some part of scripture for the doctrines which they endeavoured to propagate.

D We

We have moreover *the suffrage of professed enemies.* To require that the truth of *Moses*'s history should be attested by heathen writers of the same or nearly the same antiquity with himself would be absurd; since we know that those who affected to fix upon other nations the odious name of barbarians were in his time, and for several centuries afterwards, themselves barbarians. ¹ Yet is his authority legible in the few fragments that remain of the earliest writers, ᵐ and subsequent historians have fully confirmed it by the account which they give, though apparently mixed with depravation, of the history of the *Jews* and his legislation. With regard to the *new testament;* it is an undeniable fact that neither *Celsus, Porphyry,* nor *Julian,* nor any other who formerly wrote against *Christianity,* ever called in question the histories or the facts recorded. If they had, *the public registers of the state* would have convicted them. *That Christ did per-*

---

¹ See among others *Grotius de verit.*
ᵐ *Tacit. Justin. Diodor. Strab.*

form

form *thefe miracles*, (fays ⁿ *Juſtin Martyr* in his Apology to *Antoninus Pius*) you may know from the records that were written under *Pilate's* government. To theſe commentaries kept in the public archives *Tertullian* conſtantly and confidently appeals; which he could not have done without a certainty of being expoſed, if they had not been then extant, and the facts which he advanced therein recorded. If any one notwithſtanding ſhould think that the zealous apologiſts might quote at random, and throw the proof upon their adverſaries; let him examine *the accuſations* brought againſt the primitive Chriſtians, and their *confeſſions* before pagan tribunals; let him read carefully the account which ⁰ *Pliny*, appointed by *Trajan* to take cognizance of them, gives the emperor of their religious aſſemblies, their doctrines, and civil practices; he will in all of them find the ſubſtance of our holy religion, as contained in the evangelical and apoſtolical writings now extant. I ſhould be endleſs were I to proſecute this argument,

---

ⁿ P. 93. Ed. Oxon.   ⁰ *Plin.* l. 10. Ep. 97.

and

SERMON II.

and point out the different parts of the gospel narratives, which are so strongly confirmed both by pagan and jewish histories as necessarily to enforce and demonstrate the truth of the rest. So powerful is this evidence, and the force of it was so sensibly felt by *Julian*, one of the bitterest enemies Christianity ever had, that [p] he forbad its professors the use of profane literature; lest their apologists should foil pagans at their own weapons, and confute them out of their own authors; [q] *which method* (says *Lactantius*), *if learned men would take, false religions would quickly vanish*.

I shall not repeat what I have already said concerning *the excellency of the doctrines contained in the scriptures*; I barely now mention it for the sake of observing,

---

[p] *Amm. Marc.* xxii. 10.

[q] He finds fault with *Cyprian* for arguing with *Demetrianus* out of the scriptures which he did not believe; and observes that he ought to have produced human testimonies—those of philosophers and historians—*ut suis potissimum refutaretur auctoribus*. And then he adds—*Si hortatu nostro docti homines ac diserti huc se conferre cœperint—evanituras brevi religiones falsas et occasuram esse omnem philosophiam nemo dubitaverit. Lactant.* l. 5, c. 4.

that it is by no means confonant to reafon to fuppofe that fuch fublime and pure ideas of the nature, attributes, and worfhip of God could have been invented by a people of fuch grofs intellectuals as the Jews are well known to have been, famous for no kind of learning, utter ftrangers to philofophy and fcience, ever prone to fuperftition and idolatry. Their religion they could not borrow from their neighbours; for they were feparated from them by every diftinguifhing circumftance; by language, rites, and manner of life; nay they were by their laws abfolutely forbidden having any commerce with other nations: If this had not been the cafe, yet how could they have learned the worfhip of the only true God from thofe, who paid adoration to as many deities as there were ftars in the firmament?

The fame obfervation may be made with regard to thofe by whom *Chriftianity* was firft preached; they were mean and illiterate, fifhermen and publicans; and yet there is more true fublimity and fcience in one page of their writings than in in all the volumes of all the philosophers put together. The precepts in the mean while and injunctions were harsh, and declared open war to all worldly pleasures; the profession was attended with great self denial, perils, and sufferings. As therefore nothing less than the spirit of wisdom and revelation could discover to them a religion which exceeds all human capacity, so nothing but the invincible power of truth could induce them to adhere to it in spite of public hatred and all kinds of injuries and tortures, which malice could invent and cruelty execute^r.

---

^r When mention is made of their regard to truth, it would be unjust to forget that ingenuous honesty with which they transmit to posterity their own faults and disgraces. Witness the account which they all give of the rebellions, idolatries, and apostacies of their own nation, the noble sincerity with which *Moses* records the crimes of *his progenitor Levi*, *his sister's* murmurings, *his brother's* infamous yielding to the Israelites, and *his own* exclusion from the promised land. The *Evangelists* with the same candour relate at large the incredulity of *Thomas*, the ambition of *the sons of Zebedee*, their disputes among themselves, and their forsaking their master in the hour of danger. *Matthew* makes no secret of his odious profession; St. *Paul* frequently mentions his own furious and bloody zeal; and St. *Mark* (who is allowed to have written his gospel under the direction of St. *Peter)* takes particular notice with the addition of some aggravating circumstances of that apostle's denial of *Christ*. This ingenuity of theirs cuts off all suspicion of fraud and insincerity in all other respects.

SERMON II.

The wonderful *harmony and connection* of all the parts of scripture is no mean proof of its authority and divine original. Other *historians* differ continually from each other: the errors of the first writers are constantly criticised and corrected by succeeding adventurers, and their mistakes are sure to meet with the same treatment from those who come after them: nay, how often does it happen that cotemporary writers contradict each other in relating a fact, which has happened in their own time, within the sphere of their own knowledge? But in the scriptures there is no dissent or contradiction; the writers of a great part of them lived at very different times, and in distant places, so that there could be no confederacy or collusion; and yet their relations agree with and mutually support each other. Not only human *historians* but *philosophers*, even of the same school, disagree about their tenets; whereas the two testaments like the ˢ *two Cherubs* look stedfastly towards each other,

ˢ *Exod.* xxv. 20.

and towards the mercy-feat which they encompafs; the holy writers, men of different education, faculties, rank, and occupations; prophets, evangelifts, apoftles; notwithftanding the diverfity of time and place, the variety of matter confifting of myfteries of *providence* as well as myfteries of *faith*, yet all concur uniformly in carrying on one confiftent plan of fupernatural doctrines, all conftantly propofe the fame invariable truth flowing from the fame fountain through different channels.

As this wonderful correfpondency cannot rationally be afcribed to any other caufe than their being all dictated by the fame fpirit of wifdom and fore-knowledge, fo moreover is their (I may fay) *miraculous prefervation* a ftrong inftance of God's providential care, a conftant fanction and confirmation of the truth contained in them, continued by him without intermiffion in all ages of the church. Whence comes it that whilft the hiftories of *mighty empires* are loft in the wafte of time, the very names of their founders, conquerors, and legiflators, configned with their bodies to the

SERMON II.

the silence and oblivion of the grave: Whence comes it that the [t] history of a *mean insignificant people* and the settlement of God's church should from its very beginning, which is coeval with the world itself, to this day remain full and compleat? Whence comes it that nothing is left of innumerable volumes of philosophy and polite literature, in the preservation of which the admiration and care of all mankind seemed to conspire; and that the scriptures have in spite of all opposition come down to our time entire and genuine? During the captivity the *urim* and *thummim*, the ark itself, and every glory of the jewish worship was lost; [u] during the profanation of *Antiochus*, whosoever was found with the book of the law was put to death, and every book that could be found burned with fire: [w] the same

---

[t] There is a chasm in the Jewish history of near 250 years, viz. between the death of *Nehemiah* and the time of the *Maccabees*; but *Judea* being during that period a province of *Syria* and under the prefecture of it, the history of the Jews is of course involved in that of the country to which they were subject.—This was the case during the captivity.

[u] 1 *Macch.* i. 56, 57.

[w] Particularly in that dreadful persecution under the emperor *Diocletian* about the year 303.—See *Euseb.* l. 7.

impious

impious artifice was put in practice by several roman emperors during their persecutions of the Christians, yet have the sacred volumes survived and triumphed over these and numberless other calamities. I need not mention that more than egyptian darkness which overwhelmed religion for several centuries; during which any falsification was secure, especially in the old testament, the hebrew language being entirely unknown to all but the Jews: and yet they have, in spite of their prejudices, preserved with scrupulous care even those passages which confirm most the christian religion; the providence of God having been graciously pleased to make their blindness a standing evidence of the truth of the scriptures, their obstinacy an instrument to maintain and promote his doctrine and his kingdom. I need not remind you of the present low state of many churches, and the total annihilation of others, whereof nothing now remains but the name and the scriptures translated for their use—happy in this respect, that their particular misfortune is of service to the general cause; insomuch that

that so many copies in so many different languages, preserved under so many untoward circumstances, and differing from each other in no essential point, are a wonderful proof of their authenticity, authority, divinity.

In these proofs, though drawn from human reasoning, clear evidences appear of divine interposition, and consequently of the truth of those writings " which " are the great charter of Christians, " upon the validity of which their faith " and their hope are built." But Christianity rests not entirely upon human reasoning: God has given less equivocal attestations of its divine original; that the first preachers and propagators of it received their commission from him is manifest by the *miracles* they were enabled to perform; and that their writings were dictated by his eternal spirit, the many *prophecies* they contain, and their punctual accomplishment, abundantly demonstrate.

To answer all the objections made to *miracles* by the adversaries of our religion would

would lead me into too wide a field, and an attempt of that kind is rendered unneceſſary by the ſuccefsful labours of many pious apologiſts, who have beyond all exception ſhewn the poſſibility of them, their neceſſity, and ſufficiency towards the proofs of a divine miſſion. I ſhall only obſerve that the firſt enemies of the goſpel, *Celſus, Hierocles, Porphyry*, and *Julian*, had a very different opinion from what our modern infidels entertain of teſtifications of this kind; and therefore, though they could not deny the reality, they endeavoured to derogate from the greatneſs, of our Saviour's miracles; leſt, if they ſhould allow them in their full extent, they ſhould be forced to acknowledge the work ſupernatural, the worker omnipotent. Having thus leſſened and reduced them, they oppoſed to them miracles ſaid to have been performed by *Apuleius, Apollonius, Ariſteas,* and others whoſe names were forgotten almoſt as ſoon as mentioned; they attributed them to *art magic,* which [x] they ſaid our Savi-

---

[x] They had read or heard that *Chriſt* had been removed into *Egypt* to avoid *Herod*'s fury; but they choſe to give
another

our learned in *Egypt*—when he was two years old; ʸ to the *invocations of demons and evil spirits*—whose power and operations he came to destroy; ᶻ to the *names of powerful angels* stolen from the shrines of *Egypt*—a conceit in all probability borrowed from the *Jews*, ᵃ who asserted that his miracles were owing to the *unutterable name of God*, the *Shem Hamephorash* which he had stolen out of the temple. " ᵇ See " here the force of prejudice, the vanity " of reason, the strange perverseness of " the human mind: the heathen philo- " sophers believed magic, the *Jews* had " faith in amulets, and yet both of them " disbelieved Christianity!"

These idle pretences are solidly confuted by several of the fathers; who ᶜ among

---

another reason for this removal, and asserted that " he had " been brought up there secretly, and having thoroughly " learned *magic* returned into *Judea* and set himself up for " a God." *Celsus* apud *Orig.* l. 1. p. 10.

ʸ *Ibid.* p. 7.

ᶻ *Magus* fuit: clandestinis artibus omnia illa perfecit: *Ægyptiorum ex adytis Angelorum potentia nomina* et remotas furatus est disciplinas. *Arnob. adv. g.* l. 1.

ᵃ *Raym. pug. fid.* p. 290.

ᵇ *West on the resurrection.*

ᶜ Ὅπως ᾖ μή τις ἀντιληθῇς ἡμῖν, τί κωλύει κὴ τ̄ παρ' ἡμῖν λεγόμενον

other arguments make, even upon this occasion, use of that of *prophecy*. This was one of the characters by which the Jews were to know the *Messiah*; he was to come furnished with such special testimonials and powers from God. When *John* sent his disciples to enquire of *Christ*—ᵈ*art thou the* ὁ ἐρχόμενος *he that should come, or is it another person that we are in expectation of? he answered and said unto them, Go and shew John again those things which ye do hear and see; the blind receive their sight and the lame walk, the lepers are cleansed and the deaf hear, the dead are raised up and the poor have the gospel preached to them.* This was one of the prophetical marks of the *Messiah*; he was not only to perform miracles in general, but ᵉ these very miracles in particular which are here

---

μῶον Χριςὸν, ἄνθρωπον ἐξ ἀνθρώπων ὄντα, μαγικῇ τέχνῃ ἃς λέγομεν δυνάμεις πεποιηκέναι, ὲ δόξαι παρὰ τῦτο ψὸν Θεῦ εἶναι, τἰω ἀπόδειξιν ἤδη ποιησόμεθα, ἐ τοῖς λέγεσι πιςτύοντες, ἀλλὰ "τοῖς προφη-" τύυσι περὶν ἢ γβύισθαι κατ' ἀναγκίω πειθόμβυοι."--*Justin Mart. Apolog.* 1. p. 60.

ᵈ *Matth.* ii. 2, 3, 4, 5.

ᵉ *Isaiah* xxxv. 5. Our Saviour (says the pious and learned Mr. *Lowth* upon this place) proved himself to be the *Messias* to *John*'s disciples by appealing to this *prophecy*, as literally fulfilled in the *miracles* which he wrought.

specified

SERMON II.

specified by our Saviour. And in truth, though miracles muſt of themſelves be acknowledged by the ingenuous and unbiaſſed to be a poſitive and direct proof of a divine miſſion; yet when conſidered moreover as credentials, by which it was repeatedly declared that miſſion ſhould be atteſted, they acquire a freſh degree of efficacy and credit; being a ſolemn ratification of the evidence of God, whoſe faithfulneſs was bound to accompliſh what his knowledge had foretold.

The teſtimony of miracles viewed in this light is comprehended in that of prophecy: they prove the bleſſed *Jeſus* not only to have been a prophet ſent from God, but that very prophet *to whom all the prophets give witneſs*. And here it may not be amiſs to obſerve, that this ſolid and inſuperable argument is entirely peculiar to *Chriſtianity*; neither *Moſes* himſelf nor the *law* which he eſtabliſhed were predicted; both were made ſubſervient to, typical and prophetical of, their

Acts x. 43.

perfection

perfection and substance, the *Messiah* and his kingdom; for him was this plenitude of proof reserved, the universal attestation of every age since the foundation of the world: to all of them was *Christ* promised, that no generation might be without foundation for religious hope, those that preceded his coming be prepared to receive him, the then present confidently acknowledge, the future faithfully believe. [g] *Known to God are all his works from the beginning*; he alone has them all, past, present, and future, in one full and entire image before him: to foresee, foretel, and at the appointed time produce contingencies into actual existence is peculiar to him who, with a perfect and compleat knowledge, has the sole and absolute disposal of all events. On this ground God challenges idolaters and the objects of their worship. [h] *Shew the things that are to come hereafter that we may know that ye are Gods.* Numberless are the instances of this kind in which the inspired writers bear witness to themselves; they discover

[g] *Acts* xv. 18.   [h] *Is.* xli. 23.

SERMON II. 65

not only the origin but the fate of all nations, even of their own. God made the greateſt monarchies inſtruments not only to evince his juſtice, in the deſtruction of *Iſrael* and captivity of *Judah*, but likewiſe the impartiality of the hiſtorians who relate thoſe events, and the truth of the prophets who foretold them. The rejection of the *Meſſiah* by the Jews, their rejection by God, are predicted by all their prophets at a time when they were, and expected ever to be, his peculiar people; and the admiſſion of the Gentiles into the covenant upon their excluſion is delivered from [i] *Moſes* the firſt down to [k] *Malachi* the laſt of the prophets: theſe circumſtances are conſtantly united in the prediction, and were actually ſo in the accompliſhment, with the advent of *Chriſt:* the time of whoſe appearance upon earth was ſo ſtrongly marked that we are aſſured not only by the Evangeliſts, but by both Pagan and Jewiſh hiſtorians, that the whole nation was about that time big with the expectation of him [l] *who ſhould redeem Iſrael.*

[i] *Deuter.* xxxii. 21. [k] *Malac.* i. 11.
[l] *Luke* xxiv. 21.

E   This

This made them rebel againſt the Romans; this made them (as is obſerved by ᵐ one of their own nation) ready to follow every impoſtor, who took advantage of the times to abuſe their hopes and ſerve his own ambitious deſigns.

That the heathen world were not ſtrangers to this expectation, by whatever means it was raiſed in them, whether by tradition, the books of the Sibylls, their intercourſe with the Jews in conſequence of their diſperſion, or laſtly by the Greek verſion of the ſacred oracles—by whatever means this expectation was raiſed, that it was entertained by the Gentile world is too plain to be called in queſtion. To what other cauſe can we attribute the appearance of ſo many candidates at that time, and at no other, for ſovereignty, and the ready ſubmiſſion of the Romans who yet held the very name of king in deteſtation? ⁿ No leſs than *ſeventeen* prodigies are mentioned, by which *Auguſtus* was thought to be the perſon pointed

---

ᵐ *Joſ. hiſt.* 6. 5. *Suet. Veſp.* 4.   ⁿ *Sueton.* in *Aug.* 94.

at by the oracles for univerſal monarchy; and one in particular, a few months before his birth, at which the ſenate was ſo much alarmed as to decree that all the children born within that year ſhould be deſtroyed. ᵒ The ſame was predicted of *Tiberius* in his infancy by *Scribonius* an aſtrologer, with this remarkable addition "that he "was to reign without the enſigns of "royalty," *regnaturum quandoque ſed ſine regio inſigni*; a circumſtance ſo exactly correſponding with *Chriſt*'s lowly eſtate mentioned by the prophets, as to leave no doubt of the diviner's having ſtolen from them this idea of that extraordinary perſonage then univerſally looked for, who was indeed a king, but whoſe ᵖ *kingdom was not of this world.* ᑫ According to the opinion then prevailing (for which the old writings of the prieſts and an antient tradition was quoted) this univerſal king was to come from *Judea.* Hence thoſe extraordinary favours, of which *Philo* boaſts ſo much, ſhewn to the Jewiſh nation by all the emperors; hence the jealouſy which

---

ᵒ *Suet. Tib.* 14.   ᵖ *John* xviii. 36.
ᑫ *Tacit. hiſt.* l. 1. c. 13.   *Suet. Veſp.* 1.

Veſpaſian

SERMON II.

Vespasian conceived against his son *Titus* after his conquest of *Judea*, lest he should revolt from him and make himself emperor of the east; ʳ hence he murthered all that could be found of the lineage of *David*, that he might be sure of having no competitor in the east; and ˢ hence perhaps (for I would not be thought to lay too much stress upon presumptions of this kind) *Titus* himself, when the title seemed by these means to be rendered secure, had the appellation given him of *deliciæ humani generis* in allusion to the ᵗ *desire of all nations*, by which name the king pointed at in the oriental prophecy was characterised.

Thus much for the general expectation of the *Gentile* world about the time of our Saviour's appearance in the flesh. As for the *Jews*, the period for his coming was so clearly and precisely determined by

---

ʳ *Euseb. hist. ecclef.* l. 3. c. 12.
ˢ There are coins struck in honour of *Augustus* and *Galba* with this inscription. *Salus generis humani*. *Vindex* pressed *Galba* to assume the purple in these terms *ut humano generi assertorem ducemque se accommodaret*.
ᵗ *Hag.* ii. 7.

their

SERMON II.

their prophets, that it was impossible for them to mistake it. Accordingly we find them, from that time to the final destruction of their city and government, looking for him with the utmost eagerness and impatience; and, when that dreadful catastrophe had entirely cut off all their hopes, the pitiful evasions they made use of (some pretending that their sins had prevented his coming at the appointed time, others that he really did come but concealed himself) are a full demonstration against themselves, that in *Jesus Christ* all the characters of time, as well as others, were really and truly compleated. Of this truth the modern Rabbis are so sensible, that they [u] forbid under the penalty of a curse the people to examine the chronological prophecies, and compute from them the coming of the *Messiah*; which appeared so clearly fixed to [w] Rabbi *Nehemias*, who lived fifty years before *Christ*, that he declared the *Messiah* could not be deferred beyond those fifty years.

[u] *Cocceius quæst. et resp. jud. consid.* p. 332.
[w] *Grot. de verit.* l. 5. c. 14.

SERMON II.

The *Prophecies* indeed, thofe of *Daniel* particularly, are fo very explicit and were fo exactly fulfilled that [x] *Porphyry*, a learned Pagan of the third century, endeavoured in his writings againſt Chriſtianity to prove that they were not *prophetical* predictions of things future, but *hiſtorical* narratives of events already paſt, and publiſhed under the name of *Daniel* fome ages after the death of that prophet. But this method of invalidating prophecies is, as [y] St. *Jerom* rightly obferves, the greateſt evidence for the truth of them, [z] being entirely and confeſſedly founded upon the exactneſs of their accompliſhment. That they were not forged need no other proof than that they were and ſtill are kept and acknowledged by the Jews; and therefore [a] St. *Auſtin* imputes

---

[x] *Hieron. in proœm. ad comment. in Daniel.*
[y] Cujus impugnatio teſtimonium veritatis eſt. *Hieron. ibid.*
[z] As God obliged Balaam (ſays *Theodoret*) to *bleſs* his people whom he was come to *curſe*, ſo he turned the tongue of *Porphyry* againſt himſelf and employed him as an inſtrument to deſtroy the falſhood which he laboured to eſtabliſh. *Theodor. de curand. Græcor. affect. l. 3.*
[a] *Auguſt. Ep. 59.*

their

SERMON II. 71

their prefervation and difperfion to God's peculiar providence making good that prophetical prayer of the *Pfalmift*, [b] *flay them not left my people forget it* ; *but fcatter them abroad among the people*; that thus they might carry among all nations clear and unfufpected demonftrations, that *Jefus* whom they rejected was truly the *Meffiah* who [c] *Mofes and the prophets did fay fhould come*.

To this teftimony born to Chriftianity by the predictions of the *old teftament* we muft not forget, though ftreightened by the time ufually allotted to difcourfes of this kind, to add thofe of our *Saviour* himfelf, which were afterwards punctually verified by the event. He foretold every minute circumftance of his own fufferings, thofe of his difciples; his death, refurrection, and afcenfion; the affiftances which he would grant his Apoftles by the miffion of the Holy Ghoft, the perfecutions, the herefies, and apoftacies of his followers, and in fpite of all thefe ob-

[b] *Pf.* lix. 11.   [c] *Acts* xxvi. 22.

stacles the speedy and wonderful propagation of the gospel; *ᵈ this gospel of the kingdom shall be preached in all the world for a witness to all nations and then shall the end come*, the end or destruction of *Jerusalem* and the whole Jewish nation; which, as he told them at a time when it was very unlikely to happen, did however happen *ᵉ before that generation passed*. The dismal calamities attending it are distinctly and particularly enumerated; ᶠ the fortification by which *Titus* encompassed the city in such a manner that none could come out of it; the famine consequent thereupon; the total demolition of the temple and city; the amazing slaughter of the inhabitants; the captivity and dispersion of those that survived, circumstances all expressly mentioned in our *Saviour*'s prophecy of those days of vengeance, distress, and wrath, stand as expressly recorded in the writings of an historian of their own of undoubted credit and authority.

ᵈ *Matth.* xxiv. 14.   ᵉ *Luke* xxi. 32.
ᶠ Compare the 24th chapter of St *Matthew*, the latter part of the 19th and the 21st of St. *Luke* with *Josephus*. l. 6, 7.

Upon

Upon the whole then—Religion being (as the logicians speak) the *copula relationis* between God and man must of course be as antient as that relation. No other writings whatever besides the holy scriptures attempt any account of the *primitive religion* of the world. In them we have through the special providence of God *miraculously preserved* the several declarations of his will which he was pleased to make to our forefathers from the beginning; *every dispensation, however different in appearance, is found to be in truth and substance the same*; all through a variety of circumstances are by a wonderful concatenation made subservient to the same end, center and terminate in him who was prefigured by their rites and ceremonies, of whom all the patriarchs were types, all the priests and prophets representations. The truth of the facts recorded is proved beyond the possibility of a doubt by several internal marks, and externally *by the length of time* in which their authenticity has been allowed, by a *constant uninterrupted tradition* confirmed by *the acknowledgement of our adversaries adverfaries themfelves.* The *doctrines* by their *excellency* bear ample teftimony to themfelves. They have moreover received the fanction of *a direct and folemn attestation from heaven* " by the mediation of " figns and works fupernatural beyond the " power of any creature to effect or coun-" terfeit." Thefe works were confeffedly performed by the bleffed *Jefus,* and in his name and by his appointment by thofe alfo whom he commiffioned to carry on the great fcheme of falvation begun by himfelf. The divinity of thefe miracles themfelves are in a peculiar manner confirmed by their *having been foretold*: in him whom we acknowledge this together with all the other *prophetical marks and characters* by which the *Meffiah* was to be known exactly concur. He was to be ᵍ *born at Bethlehem,* ʰ *of the tribe of Judah, of the* ⁱ *royal houfe of David;* circumftances afcertained by the providence of God,

---

ᵍ *Micah* v. 2. *Matth.* ii. 7.

ʰ This is clearly fignified by the patriarch *Jacob. Genef.* xlix. 7. *Heb.* vii. 14.

ⁱ *Ifa.* xi. 1, 10. *Jer.* xxiii. 5, &c.—Hence our Saviour is in the *Revelations.* v. 5. called *the lion of the tribe of Judah, the root of David.*

who

who made the enrolment of the empire by a pagan fubfervient to the fulfilling and notoriety of his prophecies. He was to be [k] *born of a virgin*, and though of royal lineage yet of [l] *a poor family, of external meanness and obscurity*; [m] the latter of these circumſtances his adverſaries always urged againſt him; the former his evangeliſts and all other diſciples, perſons of unimpeached integrity, conſtantly avowed; and had the truth thereof not been notorious, the inquiſitive malice of the Scribes and Phariſees would ſoon have detected and gladly publiſhed the falſhood. [n] He was to come, according to the patriarch *Jacob*, while the tribe of *Judah* and thoſe who adhered to it remained one body politic governed by their own laws; according to the prophets [o] *Haggai* and [p] *Malachi* while the ſecond temple ſtood; according to the prediction of [q] *Daniel* ſhortly before the

---

[k] *Iſa.* vii. 14. *Matth.* i. 23.
[l] *Iſa.* xlix. 7. liii. 3.
[m] *Is not this the carpenter, the ſon of Mary, the brother of James &c?—And they were offended at him.* Mark vi. 3.— *Matth.* xiii. 55, &c.
[n] *Geneſ.* xlix. 8.
[o] *Hagg.* ii. 6, 7, 8.
[p] *Mal.* iii. 1.
[r] *Dan.* ix. 24, 26.

deſtruction

destruction of the city and sanctuary, within a determined period of time, which, however computed, falls within the compass of the age wherein he lived and the destruction of *Jerusalem*. To prepare the Jews for this period God had been pleased to wean them by degrees from the law of *Moses:* he built them indeed a temple after the captivity; but withdrew the ark of his presence and the *urim* and *thummim* from among them, and accepted of offerings made by strange fire; thus abrogating one ceremony after the other as the time approached wherein *Christ* was to cancel all the ordinances. When he appeared upon earth he confirmed what the prophet had foretold concerning the abomination of desolation, the demolition of this second temple, their woeful tragedy, captivity and dispersion. It accordingly came to pass, and then their peculiarity visibly ceased; their polity both civil and ecclesiastical was totally destroyed; and they have ever since remained miserable exiles, without the distinction of tribes or genealogies, ' *without prince,*

' *Song of the three children.* v. 14.

SERMON II.

prophet or leader, without burnt-offering, sacrifice, oblation, incense, or place to sacrifice before God. That polity, during the continuance of which *Shiloh* was to come, is now diffolved; the temple, which *the defire of all nations* was to fill with his glory, is laid even with the ground; the period, in which the *Meffiah* was to make an atonement for fin, is expired; and the whole nation of the Jews a ftanding monument of the ˢ defolation which was to come at the end thereof. If therefore the *Meffiah* foretold by the prophets be not already come, he can never come; the place, the time, and all other circumftances affigned to him, are now no more. But the *Meffiah* foretold by the prophets is come, and therefore is ᵗ *the vifion and prophecy fealed up*; all the predictions of foregoing ages concerning him are accomplifhed, and therefore neither the place, nor the time, nor any other circumftance affigned to him is or can be any more. ᵘ *Wherefore holy brethren partakers of the*

ˢ *Dan.* ix. 26.   ᵗ *Dan.* ix. 24.   ᵘ *Heb.* iii. 1.

heavenly

heavenly calling let us not ^w *rebel against the light,* ^x *let us take heed lest there be in any of us an evil heart of unbelief;* for ^y *how shall we escape, if we neglect so great salvation, which at the first began to be spoken by the Lord, and has been confirmed unto us by them that heard him; God also bearing them witness both with signs and wonders and with divers miracles and gifts of the Holy Ghost?*

^w *Job* xxiv. 13.   ^x *Heb.* iii. 12.   ^y *Heb.* ii. 3, 4.

SERMON III.

ISAIAH lxi. 1, 2.

The Spirit of the Lord is upon me; because the Lord hath anointed me to preach good tidings unto the meek; he hath sent me to bind up the broken-hearted, to proclaim liberty to the captives, and the opening of the prison to them that are bound; to proclaim the acceptable year of the Lord.

[a]THERE have not been wanting men of piety and abilities who have endeavoured to overthrow the *evangelical*

---
[a] See Mr. *Lowth*'s excellent preface to his learned Commentaries on the prophets.

sense of the prophecies of the old testament, confining them merely to what is improperly called their primary meaning, and appropriating them wholly to the persons of whom or to whom they were proximately spoken, and their accomplishment to or near the times in which they were delivered.

It may indeed be doubted whether the prophets themselves fully understood the chief and ultimate design of [b] *what they spake when they were moved by the Holy Ghost*; but it is matter of astonishment that any intelligent and unprejudiced reader of the scriptures can call into question the typical meaning of the prophecies, which those authentic records assure him were fulfilled in the promised *Messiah*.

[c] The space of time from *Isaiah* to *Malachi* was surely too narrow a boundary

---

[b] 2 *Pet.* ii. 21.
[c] *Isaiah*'s first vision was in the year that king *Uzziah* died. c. vi. 1. *Malachi* was cotemporary, if not the same, with *Ezra*: the space between them can therefore but very little, if at all, exceed three hundred years.

SERMON III.

to confine the plenitude of divine revelation; the captivity of the Jews and their return from thence, though under the direction of Providence, were certainly of themselves events too inconsiderable to merit all the pomp and solemnity with which the visions are introduced and the actors in that glorious scene, even Cherubim and Seraphim and the God of *Israel* himself. Such special interpositions could not have temporary occurrences only for their objects, but through them extended their view to ^d *what should come to pass at the last, and shewed what should come to pass for ever.* The exultation and triumph of the prophetical promises were particularly designed to raise in the minds of the Jews an expectation of far greater blessings than their deliverance from the *Babylonish* captivity, and return to *Judea*. These were only preludes to their deliverance from the dominion of sin, and title to the *heavenly Canaan*; blessings, which such among them as believed have obtained, and we through the tender mercy of our God this

^d *Eccluf.* xlviii. 24, 25.

day enjoy. And accordingly we read throughout the infpired writings that the Apoftles looked upon *the teftimony of Jesus* to be *the spirit of prophecy*; always confirming, when they difputed with the Jews, the doctrines of the *new* by the writings of the *old teftament*. But we have ftill greater authority than theirs, even that of our bleffed Saviour; who in his expofition of the prophecy, which I have chofen for my text, has applied it to himfelf faying after he had read it—*This day is fulfilled ἡ γραφὴ αὕτη ἐν τοῖς ὠσὶν ὑμῶν this very fcripture which you have juft now heard.*

The prophet *Isaiah* from whom the words are taken, having in the foregoing chapters defcribed under feveral *fymbols* and *allegories* the fate of the church from the beginning to the end of time, at laft introduces the *Meffiah* manifefting himfelf to the Jewifh nation, and explaining his own office together with the benefits and privileges of the oeconomy of grace in *familiar phrafes* by an eafy allufion to a

---

Revel. xix. 10.   *Luke* iv. 21.

solemn festival, designed to put them in mind of a *temporal* and prefigure a *spiritual* deliverance. This was the ᵍ *Jubilee* celebrated with the greatest tokens of joy by God's own express appointment; every particular circumstance of which was analogous to some part of the gospel dispensation, and the whole a lively adumbration of the ʰ *mercy promised to our forefathers through the redemption that is in Christ Jesus.*

God in the beginning created man upright, and bestowed upon him many singular marks of especial regard and favour, dignifying him with the prerogative of dominion over the rest of the creation, and placing him in a delightful garden which he honoured with his own immediate presence, condescending to have frequent intercourse with man. The tree of life was planted in the midst; the fruit of which was appointed by a *natural* or *sacramental* virtue to preserve and prolong his life in this state of bliss and glory.

ᵍ *Levit.* 25.   ʰ *Luke* i. 72. *Rom.* iii. 24.

But he was disobedient to the divine command, and eat of the only fruit which God had forbidden him, having expressly said, *in the day that thou eatest thereof thou shalt surely die.* In the penalty of death annexed to disobedience was virtually implied the promise of life upon obedience; but the conditions of the covenant being broken, all title to the reward was forfeited; the punishment denounced must be inflicted, or the honour of the law and the authority of the lawgiver trampled upon. The covenant had been by the goodness of God accommodated in every respect to the nature of man; his reason and understanding, his appetites and passions, were interested in his obedience: *the injunction of a positive command* was founded on that duty, which reason could not but tell him he owed to his creator and benefactor; the *promise* had an especial regard to the desire of happiness interwoven in his very frame; and the *threatning* to the

---

[i] *Gen.* ii. 17.
[k] This is proved at large by our excellent bishop *Bull* in his learned *discourse concerning the first covenant and the state of man before the fall.*

prevailing

prevailing affection of fear, which starts at every object destructive of his being. If after so signal and ungrateful an abuse of God's kindness man had gone totally unpunished, what idea could he have formed to himself of God's veracity, purity, and abhorrence of iniquity? Would not an absolute and unconditional pardon of this first, and therefore most heinous sin as being the cause and origin of all subsequent ones—would it not have occasioned security under guilt, and made man say in his heart, [1] *Tush the Lord does not see, neither does God regard it?* Would it not have destroyed the necessity of religion and holiness, and frustrated the solemnity of divine laws and divine commands? for if pardon is arbitrary, punishment must likewise be arbitrary; and every thing of course resolved into the despotic power of God, which necessarily supersedes if not totally annihilates his truth, justice, mercy, and other essential attributes. Man was amply provided for a continuance in his original rectitude,

---

[1] *Pf.* xciv. 7.

furnished

furnished with powers sufficient to perform the most spiritual obedience; he could therefore plead no excuse, neither could God consistently with his righteousness and veracity dispense with so direct a violation of his positive command, but was obliged to vindicate the sacredness of his laws by putting into execution the punishment denounced against the transgression.

To apprehend rightly the nature, and consequently form a true judgement, of this punishment we must consider it in *three* distinct points of view; for the death denounced in the sentence is *threefold.*—First, *A spiritual death,* a deprivation of that purity and holiness derived from the divine image imprinted on the soul of man.—Secondly, *A temporal death,* a subjection to the miseries of a corrupt and depraved nature, to labour and pain, infirmities and diseases, and at last a separation of the soul from the body.—Thirdly, *An eternal death,* a future state of endless misery in the separation of the soul from God. All these kinds of death were included

SERMON III.

cluded in the penalty annexed to the violation of the covenant of works. But ᵐ *God had not forgotten to be gracious;* ⁿ *in the midst of wrath he remembered mercy:* of the *three* parts of which the punishment consisted the *first* only was immediately felt. And this perhaps may not so properly be said to have been a punishment inflicted as the natural effect of a natural cause, not so much a *judicial* as a *necessary* consequence of man's disobedience. There is no ° *communion between light and darkness*, neither could holiness dwell in what was sinful and corrupt. Man having once parted with his innocence, his thoughts, desires, and affections, his whole frame and constitution, became disordered and vitiated; and this degeneracy and depravity was, by the natural law of propagation, unavoidably transmitted by him to his unhappy posterity. This I apprehend to be the true meaning of what is called *original sin*, the absence of original righteousness; that darkness in the understanding

ᵐ *Pf.* lxxvii. 9.   ⁿ *Habak.* iii. 2.
° 2 *Cor.* vi. 14.

and

and obliquity in the will, which succeeded that original light and rectitude by which *Adam*, if he had continued in his obedience, would have been enabled to have led *a spiritual life* here on earth; but, having suffered himself to be despoiled of them by the wiles of the tempter, both he and those, who with their being derived the infection from him, became *spiritually dead,* ᵖ *dead in trespasses and sins.*

This sad effect of their disobedience our first parents, I say, immediately and very severely felt : ᵠ *they knew that they were naked*; they perceived the foul degradation of their nature and ʳ *hid themselves from the presence of the Lord God.* Consciousness of their guilt brought upon them the dread of God's just anger and resentment, and anticipated all the horrors and torments of punishment even before sentence was pronounced.

The other parts of the penalty though God did not, could not, absolutely dis-

---
ᵖ *Ephes.* ii. 1. ᵠ *Genes.* iii. 7.
ʳ *Genes.* iii. 8.

pense

penfe with; yet he did not directly or rigoroufly exact them; he granted the offenders a long reprieve from *temporal* death, and even before he paffed fentence conveyed to them by the promife of a redeemer the comfortable hopes of their being totally delivered from *eternal* death, and recovering the title to life which they had forfeited by their difobedience. That *Adam* underftood the promife in this fenfe is, I think, plain from his changing the name of his wife, and henceforth calling her *Eve*; clearly alluding to the promifed ˢ *feed of the woman* by whom all mankind (now under fentence of death) were to be reftored to life. And that *Eve*'s hopes likewife were erect is evident from her fond and fanguine expectation of this great deliverer in her firft-born. ᵗ *I have gotten*, fays fhe, *a man from the Lord*; or as ᵘ fome learned men (who think that in the original the particle את denotes, as it

---

ˢ *Genef.* iii. 20.   ᵗ *Genef.* iv. 1.
ᵘ Among others *Ifidorus Clarius*, who adds, *Nam et cabaliftica traditio meminit promiffionis de Meffiah primis parentibus factæ*. See *Berriman*'s fourth fermon at Boyle's lectures and the authorities he quotes.

often

often does, the accusative case) render the words by apposition, *I have gotten the Man-God.*

Together with moral, physical evil also was introduced into the world; whether by a natural connexion between them arising from the original constitution of things, or by a special interposition of providence at this period, lies within the bosom of the Almighty; but that the earth did actually sympathize with man, and that the promise of deliverance from corruption was expected to extend to the material world, the prophecy of *Lamech* at the birth of *Noah*, the typical restorer of mankind, is a direct and positive proof. He gave him the name of *Noah* which signifies *comfort* saying, " *this same shall comfort us concerning our work and toil of our hands because of the ground which the Lord hath cursed.* God whose every dispensation is founded on mercy, and has always a respect to that amazing instance of it the redemption of man through

^w *Genes.* v. 29.

Christ,

SERMON III.

Chrift, was pleafed to keep this affurance alive by various methods, by promifes declaratory and emblematical; never leaving his fallen creatures without hope, nor his gracious intentions without witnefs. [x] That he continued to favour them with feveral, if not manifeftations of his prefence, at leaft revelations of his will has been concluded from fome hints given by *Mofes* in his fhort hiftory of mankind before the flood. Of this point the prophecy of *Lamech* juft mentioned feems to me clearly decifive. It is however worthy of obfervation that he makes mention only of the curfe, which the Lord had pronounced and inflicted on the ground; whereas *Adam's* prophetical impofition of the name of *Eve* upon his wife has plainly a refpect only to the reftoration of mankind to life by the promifed feed. It feems therefore not unreafonable to fuppofe that there had been a fubfequent revelation, in which God made known his gracious purpofe of relieving man's temporal mifery, by an abatement of that fterility, malignity, and

---

[x] See *Shuckford's connection*, l. 1.

general

general depravation which had on the fall infected the whole inanimate creation. *Adam* poſſibly might not feel this part of the curſe in its full rigour; that it was encreaſed upon the murder of *Abel* is more than probable; for *the* [y] *Lord ſaid unto Cain, When thou tilleſt the ground it ſhall not* henceforth *yield unto thee her ſtrength*; which words ſurely imply that it had hitherto in ſome degree yielded her ſtrength, in a degree ſuperior to that in which it ſhould do it for the future. As men increaſed in wickedneſs we may, from the analogy eſtabliſhed between moral and phyſical evil, venture to ſuppoſe that the curſe increaſed in proportion, till at laſt impiety having attained its utmoſt height it was fully compleated by the total deſtruction of the earth.

When *Noah* took poſſeſſion of the new world his father's prophecy began to take place.—[z] *The Lord ſaid in his heart, I will*

---

[y] *Geneſ.* iv. 12. For this obſervation and others adopted in this diſcourſe I am indebted to Dr. *Worthington*'s *Eſſay on Redemption.*

[z] *Geneſ.* viii. 21.

SERMON III.

not again curse the ground any more for man's sake.—While the earth remaineth, seed time and harvest, and cold and heat, and summer and winter, and day and night, shall not cease, plainly intimating that ªthe temperature of the air and the variety of seasons, which by their irregularity were instruments of correction in the antediluvian world, should for the future by their regularity and constant succession be instruments of mercy, and the means of removing that curse of which the flood had been the effect and consequence.

Noah being typical of our Saviour and the deluge of baptism the blessings, contained in the covenant made with him in consequence of the flood, are likewise typical of the blessings promised by the evangelical covenant in consequence of our spiritual regeneration by the waters of baptism. But the type is always inferior to the antitype; the blessings covenanted

---

ª See Bishop *Sherlock*'s *fourth discourse on prophecy*, and his *second dissertation* annexed to the discourses.

with

with *Noah* were merely temporal, and even that in a lower degree; by them indeed the severity of the curse was greatly softened, but by no means totally removed: yet did this relief administer great comfort upon his entrance into the new world; it was a pledge of and a prelude to the restitution of nature to its original state, in the same manner as *Enoch* was to his forefathers an earnest of their deliverance from that far greater penalty of the curse, subjection unto death.

Thus did God by different revelations at different periods preserve man from despair, and provide for his present comfort by giving him frequent assurances that he should in time be raised from that deplorable degradation into which he was sunk, and restored to his primitive righteousness and of course to his primitive happiness. For there is, as we have before observed, a correspondence between moral and physical evil; the world, having been made for man, felt together with man the effects of God's displeasure; it fell,

fell, and by confequential reafoning will rife with man; it has been made an inftrument of mifery to fin, and will by the bleffing of God be made an inftrument of felicity to righteoufnefs; when according to the eftablifhed rules of its fubferviency to moral caufes it fhall hereafter together with man recover its former excellence and perfection: [b] *Thou fhalt judge the folk righteoufly and govern the nations upon earth: then fhall the earth bring forth her increafe, and God even our own God fhall give us his bleffing.*

The removal of the curfe is with great probability fuppofed to have commenced immediately after the deluge, and continued ever fince by flow degrees in proportion to man's advancement in virtue and piety. And hence I prefume may in fome meafure be conceived one reafon why God, in his dealings with our forefathers, made *temporal* rewards and punifhments the only fanctions of his laws. The whole fcheme of redemption was too ex-

[b] *Pf.* lxvii. 4. 6.

SERMON III.

tensive and sublime to be comprehended by men, whose intellectual as well as moral faculties had not yet recovered the shock they had received by the fall; the mysteries therefore of a *spiritual* deliverance (though by far the most excellent part, nay, properly speaking the whole of the promise because *natural* blessings are the genuine effects and necessary consequence of *spiritual* ones) the mysteries, I say, of a *spiritual* deliverance, not being accommodated to the infirmities of an infant capacity, were not fully revealed; but suggested only by general hints, represented by personal types, and shadowed under ceremonial figures: whereas the removal of temporal evils, the sad effects of which they could not but perceive and feel, being more likely to operate upon them was expressly made the ^c basis

---

^c *If ye walk in my statutes and keep my commandments and do them, then I will give you rain in due season, and the land shall yield her increase, &c. &c.* Levit. xxvi. 3, 4. &c.—On the contrary, disobedience was threatened with temporal punishments.—*But if ye will not hearken unto me, and will not do all these commandments; I will also do this unto you; I will even appoint over you terror, &c. I will bring the land into desolation.* ibid. 14. 16. 32. This curse was afterwards on account of their disobedience carried into execution, and

of all covenants and the reward of their obedience: God even by this method still carrying on in an efficacious, though secret, manner his gracious plan of making the recovery of the *natural* the consequence of the restoration of the *moral* world. For this gradual reparation of the breaches made in nature (exclusive of the powerful motives to virtue and piety, which the proportion it bore to their obedience supplied them with) could not but raise and cherish in them a comfortable confidence, not only that they would at last be totally closed up, but that the other part also of the promise would in God's own time have its full completion.

To keep this confidence alive and support men in their state of mortality with the hopes of a restoration to life, God

---

and remains *visibly* in full force even to this day; bearing ample testimony to the veracity of God, and consequently affording hope and assurance that (as he has *turned a fruitful land into barrenness for their wickedness* so, likewise) *when they follow after righteousness and seek the Lord, he will comfort Zion; he will comfort all her waste places, and he will make her wilderness like Eden, and her desert like the garden of the Lord.* *Is.* li. 1. 3.

G   had

had been pleased (as has been before observed) to give them an earnest and pledge of it in *Enoch,* and he afterwards renewed it in *Elijah*; both of whom were on account of their exemplary lives translated from this world without tasting death. Yet, notwithstanding these notices, and the insight which the more enlightened among them had into the spiritual meaning of the types, figures, and promises, (of which whoever reads the 11th chapter to the *Hebrews* with attention can have no doubt) yet the generality of them seem not to have had any other idea of the redemption by the *Messiah,* than that of a temporal or earthly redemption. It was the gospel alone that *ᵈ brought immortality to light*; *ᵉ to the promises of the life that now is* adding the promises of *that which is to come.* Even the *Prophets* themselves, though in their days the oeconomy of grace was very much opened and unfolded, seem not in their promises to reach beyond the grave; the blessings contained in their predictions stop short of eternity;

ᵈ 2 *Tim.* i. 10.   ᵉ 1 *Tim.* iv. 8.

they all appear to tend to, center and terminate in, that ἀποκατάστασις πάντων [f] *that restitution of all things,* which St. *Peter* assures us *God hath spoken by the mouth of all his holy prophets since the world began;* [g] *for which the earnest expectation of the creature waiteth;* to which the whole creation, animate and inanimate, sensitive and rational, progressively aspires.

Some fragments of this doctrine are to be found in both Jewish and Heathen antiquity. It was a favourite dogma of the eastern and greek philosophers, especially those of the *Pythagorean* and *Platonic* schools; from the last of which the period in which it was expected to happen was called the *Platonic year* [h]. An opinion, said

---

[f] *Acts* iii. 21.   [g] *Rom.* viii. 19.

[h] It was likewise held by the *Stoics*; and indeed its universality has been incontestibly proved by an ingenious writer of our own in his learned, though fanciful, *theory of the new heavens and the new earth.* From whatever source it was derived to the more ancient philosophers, the later Romans in all probability borrowed it from the Jews; since *Virgil* in his famous *Eclogue* assigns to it the very same period that the Jews did, viz.—*the advent of the Messiah:* though the Jews by so doing evidently confound the *two advents* mentioned by their prophets.

to have been handed down from *Elias*, prevailed much among the Jews that this blessed state would take place and be accomplished in the seventh millenary; and of this *septenary* state of rest, joy, and triumph they conceived their [i] *sabbaths* to be figurative. *The Sabbath*, saith *Zoar* on *Genesis*, *The Sabbath what is it? A figure of the land of the living*, i. e. *of the world or age to come, the age of souls, the age of consolations*, meaning thereby, according to the known idiom of the Jewish language, the days of the *Messiah*; who was always spoken of by them as *the comforter and the consolation of Israel*. *The observation of the Sabbath*, says [k] another great master in *Israel, is founded upon faith in God; for no one will observe the Sabbath, except he that confesses that the world will be renovated, and that he will renovate it who created it out of nothing*.

Ipse opifex rerum, mundi melioris origo;

as the [l] *Roman* mythologist, not without

---

[i] See *Whitby* on *Heb.* iv. 9.
[k] D. *Kimchi* on *If.* lvi. 6.
[l] *Ovid. Metam.* l. 1.

copying

copying after some *Jewish* original, very expressively stiles him.

But the *Jubilee*, or sabbath of years, being the greatest of the typical revolutions was therefore looked upon as more particularly figurative of the grand *Sabbatism* of the people of God. The *Messiah*, cry all the Rabbies with one voice, *redeemeth on a Jubilee*. ᵐ *In a Jubilee the Shechinah will be redemption, ransom, and ending of sabbatism to Israel.* Accordingly if the computation made by Archbishop *Usher* be a just one, it was on a year of *Jubilee*, the very last before the total destruction of the Jewish polity, that our blessed Saviour preached the glad tidings of salvation. On that year he entered upon his prophetic office, and having read in the synagogue the passage out of the prophet *Isaiah* which I have before recited, and which describes the *Messiah* as proclaiming the

---

ᵐ *Zoar* on *Gen.* See Bishop *Patrick's Commentary* on *Levit.* 25. *Zoar* or *Zohar* is a cabalistical commentary on the law, to which the Jews ascribe great antiquity making it older than the *Talmud.* It is however by some learned men supposed to have been written by *R. Perets* in the 13th century.

Jubilee,

Jubilee, he shut the book and said, *This day is this scripture fulfilled*.

The *Jubilee* was the most considerable of all the solemnities which God enjoined to the Israelites. It was *a year of rest*, they were neither to sow nor to reap; *of liberty*, all slaves were released; *of restitution of every thing to its pristine state*, all debts were remitted, and all lands however alienated restored to their original proprietor. It began on the *day of expiation*, a day of fasting, humiliation, and confession of sins; therefore a time of penitence: [n] *it brought men back*, says Maimonides, *to their primitive state which is the effect of repentance*. And who knows not that *repentance* is the first evangelical duty? It was the sum and substance of what our Saviour's fore-runner preached as preparatory to the reception of the gospel, [o] *repent, for the kingdom of heaven is at hand*; what our Saviour himself first enjoined [p] *repent and believe the gospel*: it is always

---

[n] *Maim. de pœnâ.* c. 7.   See *Voisin de jubilæo*.
[o] *Matth.* iii. 2.   [p] *Mark* i. 15.

mentioned previous to the remission of sins as an indispensible condition for obtaining mercy, *it behoved,* says St. Luke, ^q *that repentance and remission of sins should be preached in his name.* The analogy between the *remission of debts* in the Jubilee and the *remission of sins* under the gospel covenant is obvious to every understanding; and the release of all slaves, the total cessation of the toil and labour of agriculture, and the restoration of every man to his possessions, tribe, and family, were plainly symbolical of that *acceptable year of the Lord,* wherein man was to be delivered from the servitude he was held under by sin and Satan, and restored to all the blessings which had been lost by the fall. If a Hebrew had sold himself to a stranger or proselyte, even he had the benefit of the Jubilee; but a price was to be paid for his redemption, by himself if he was able; if not, ^r *one of his brethren,* says the law, *may redeem him.* ^s *This Redeemer,* says R. Bechai, *is the Messiah the son of David of the*

---

^q *Luke* xxiv. 47. ^r *Levit.* xxv. 48.
^s *Patrick, ibid.*

tribe of Judah, that blessed Redeemer, who to free us from the obligation of the law became obedient to the law, and therefore condescended to take our nature upon him that he might have a legal right, the right of *consanguinity*, to redeem us.

The restoration of every part of nature in consequence of this redemption, thus shadowed out under this solemnity, is clearly and without all ambiguity predicted by all the prophets. " ' The kingdom " of *Christ* in this world being arrived to " its full extent and growth; truth and " peace, charity and justice, the true faith, " the sincere piety, the generous and un- " affected virtue which Christianity teaches " and prescribes, shall reign and flourish " over all the earth." ᵘ *He that is left in Zion and he that remaineth in Jerusalem shall be called holy, even every one that is written among the living in Jerusalem:* ʷ *the people shall be all righteous;* ˣ *the iniquity of Israel*

ᵗ *Scott's Christian life.*   ᵘ *Is.* iv. 3.
ʷ *Is.* lx. 21.   ˣ *Jerem.* l. 20.

shall

shall be sought for, and there shall be none; and the sins of Judah, and they shall not be found; ʸ *for God will set his sanctuary in the midst of them for evermore; his tabernacle shall be also with them, and he will dwell with them, and he will be their God and they shall be his people.*

When *man* is thus restored to his original holiness, the *earth* likewise will recover its original fertility; for as it was *cursed* with man so will it also be *blessed* with man. ᶻ *The wilderness and solitary place shall be glad, and the desert shall rejoice and blossom as the rose:* ᵃ *the plowman shall overtake the reaper, and the treader of grapes him that soweth the seed:* ᵇ *the mountains shall drop new wine, and the hills shall flow with milk:* ᶜ *God will hear the heavens, and they shall hear the earth, and the earth shall hear the corn, and the wine, and the oil.* With this outward prosperity are always joined universal benevolence, peace, and harmony; and the whole is attributed to an increase

---

ʸ *Ezech.* xxxvii. 26, 27.   ᶻ *Is.* xxxv. 1.
ᵃ *Am.* ix. 13.   ᵇ *Joel* iii. 18.
ᶜ *Hos.* ii. 21, 22.

of knowledge in the duties of religion and advancement in the practice of holiness. *[d] They shall not hurt nor destroy in all my holy mountain, for the earth shall be full of the knowledge of the Lord as the waters cover the sea; for the work of righteousness shall be peace, and the effect of righteousness quietness and assurance for ever.*

These passages were understood in their natural and literal meaning, not only by the Jews, but [e] by the most learned and orthodox Christians in the ages immediately following the apostles; [f] but the *literal* interpretation and the doctrine contained in it at length lost ground, the professors of it having the odious charge of *Judaism* fixed upon them by some warm men, who were too fond of introducing on all occasions allegorical and spiritual refinement. But why did they not charge St. *Peter* likewise with *Judaism*, who writing to the Jews declares in plain terms

---

[d] *If.* xi. 9.—xxxii. 17.
[e] *Papias, Justin Martyr, Irenæus, Apollinarius, Tertullian, Victor, Lactantius.*
[f] See Mr. *Mede.*

his

his expectation of this blessed state? God had said by his prophet *Isaiah*, ^g *Behold I create a new heaven and a new earth;* and the apostle clearly confesses his understanding him according to the plain and natural import of the words, when speaking of the real and substantial changes brought by the Lord upon the *material* world he adds, ^h *But according to his promise we also do expect new heavens and a new earth.* Why was not the same objection made to St. *John*, who " in a plain and " simple narration free from allegory and " involution of prophetical figures," not only alludes to but quotes the description given by the prophet of the happiness of this renovated world? ⁱ *They shall hunger no more, neither thirst any more—God shall wipe away all tears from their eyes, and there shall be no more death neither sorrow*

---

^g *If.* lxv. 17. In what sense the Jews understood this prophecy is plain from *R. Saadiah Gaon* as quoted by Dr. *Whitby* on 2 St. *Pet.* iii. 13. *In the end of the world there shall be to the Jews a world full of joy and exultation, so that their heaven and earth shall be as it were new.*

^h 2 *Pet.* iii. 13.

ⁱ *If.* xxv. 8.—xlix. 10.—lxv. 19. *Revel.* vii. 15.—xxi. 4.

nor crying, neither shall there be any more pain. There cannot be plainer words or expressed in a more ordinary manner; and yet they must be allegorized before the removal of those infirmities under which nature labours can be denied. Those that do it seem to me to be guilty of the same error with the Jews by applying that to the [k] *first* which is meant of the *second* coming of *Christ*; with this difference however that whereas the *Jews* will admit of no *Messiah* whose reign does not entirely consist of external splendor and temporal power; these *Christians* on the contrary banish from their idea of *Christ's* kingdom every circumstance that does not exactly

---

[k] The old prophets (for the most part) speak of the coming of *Christ* indefinitely and altogether without that distinction of the *first* and *second* coming which the gospel out of *Daniel* hath taught us. And so consequently they spake of the things to be at *Christ's* coming indefinitely and altogether; which we, who are now more fully informed by the revelation of the gospel of a twofold coming, must apply each of them to its proper time; those things that befit the state of his *first* coming unto it, and such things as befit the state of his *second* coming unto his second; and what befits both alike may be applied unto both. *Mede.* This distinction is remarked and urged by *Justin Martyr* in several parts of his dialogue with *Trypho* a Jew.

coincide

coincide with the mean and lowly appearance of the son of man. But why should the prophecies concerning our Saviour's abasement and humiliation be always taken *literally*, and those that foretel his exaltation and glorious appearance be never understood but in a *figurative* sense? Ought we not rather, as we have seen the former punctually verified, be from thence inspired with hope and confidence that the latter likewise will in God's own time be exactly accomplished? Far be it from me to suppose that there is no spiritual meaning couched under the letter; but while we allegorize every passage, and confine all the prophecies absolutely and without exception to the first advent of *Christ*, are we not in some measure partakers of the crime of those [1] *scoffers* who St. *Peter* tells us *shall come in the last days, saying, Where is the promise of his coming? for since the fathers fell asleep all things continue as they were from the beginning of the creation?* [m] do we

---

[1] 2 *Pet.* iii. 3, 4.
[m] See *univ. hist. vol.* iii. p. 39.—*Mede's works*, p. 670. To suppose those prophecies (which foretel *the visibility and universality of Christ's church, accompanied with perfect peace, prosperity and holiness,* and those which foretel *the flourishing*

110   SERMON III.

not by so doing join issue with the Jews, and confirm them in their obstinacy and infidelity?

Very different was the Apostle's method of arguing with them—[n] *repent ye and be converted* εἰς τὸ ἐξαλειφθῆναι τὰς ἁμαρτίας ὑμῶν *for the blotting out of your sins* ὅπως ἂν *that so the times of refreshing* ἀναψύξεως *of rest or comfort may come from the presence of the Lord, and that he may send Jesus Christ, which before was preached unto you, whom the heavens must receive until the times of* " restitution of all things." These times are here as in all the writings of the

---

flourishing state of the Jewish church and nation) to have already received their utmost completion is, in my judgement, to give too great an advantage to the Jews and in effect to acknowledge that they never were, nor will be fulfilled in *their natural and obvious* sense. Whereas on the other side to assert that many prophecies relating to the *Messiah* are already fulfilled in our *Lord Jesus Christ*—and withal to maintain that several others relate to his *second coming* and their accomplishment shall usher in or accompany that his glorious appearance.—I say, the observing this distinction-effectually answers all the arguments which the *Jews* make use of to support themselves in their incredulity; it discovers a perfect harmony and correspondence between the prophecies of the *old* and *new* testament, &c. *Lowth's preface.*

[n] *Acts* iii. 19, &c. See *Mede, Hammond, Raphelius.*

prophets

prophets made to coincide with the coming of *Christ*, and described as the effect and consequence of the repentance and conversion of the Jews; upon which the gentiles flowing in ° *all the ends of the world shall remember and turn unto the Lord, and all the kindreds of the nations shall worship before him.* That this flourishing estate of the church was not absolutely and fully to take place at our Saviour's first coming, is evident from his instructing his disciples to pray to God that his *kingdom* might *come*; for " that which is to come may " indeed be in its progress, but has not " yet attained to that state of perfection " which it is to have." But that it will take place before the resurrection is, I think, likewise evident; because St. *Paul* tells us that immediately after the resurrection ᵖ *Christ shall deliver up the kingdom to God, even the father.*

Then indeed will be totally compleated that glorious scheme of redemption, which has been gradually working ever since

---

° *Pf.* xxii. 27.   ᵖ 1 *Cor.* xv. 24.

man's

man's unhappy fall: God, whose *tender mercies are over all his works*, has never forgotten that upon a review of them he was pleased to pronounce them to be good; he will restore them all to their primitive beauty and perfection; but above all will he remember man the lord of the creation, and reinstate him in the full possession of that happiness, and those high privileges which he enjoyed during his innocence; with this gracious addition that, whereas eternal life was only implied in the covenant of *nature*, it is in the covenant of *grace* through the sufferings and merits of our blessed Saviour clearly revealed and expresly promised: for *where sin abounded grace did much more abound*.

The capacities of man as an individual are progressive; so are those of human nature taken collectively; and God has always been pleased to accommodate his dispensations to this law of progression:

q *Pf.* cxlv. 9. r *Rom.* v. 20.
s See my late learned and pious friend Dr. *Durell's* dissertation on the character of the patriarch *Abraham*.

SERMON III:

he brings mankind from nature to grace, from grace to glory. We (to bring at laſt this diſcourſe to ourſelves) are in a ſtate of grace, in a middle ſtate between nature and glory, and therefore though ſtill in a great degree ſubject to the infirmities of the one, yet at the ſame time enlightened with ſome rays reflected from the other. We have received the gift of faith ‘*the firſt fruits of the ſpirit*; yet much of corruption cleaves to us; our original ſin, though pardoned, is as yet but imperfectly purged: we are not yet arrived to that bleſſed ſtate which is promiſed, when all evil both *natural* and *moral* ſhall be totally removed; yet that they are greatly abated no one can deny without doing violence to his own experience compared with the hiſtories of former times. The earth, thanks be to God, bears her fruit in due ſeaſon, neither does the general face of it bear many marks of that curſe which prevented it " *when it was tilled from yielding her ſtrength*. Though the

˒ *Rom.* viii. 23. ᵘ *Gen.* iv. 12.

practice of universal righteousness, which is the design of the gospel, is far from being established; we do not however find that mankind in general gives into those abominable excesses, of which, to the disgrace of human nature, history both *sacred* and *profane* records such frequent examples. That the influence of Christianity with regard to its most distinguishing character is not totally lost, that spirit of benevolence which is visible in our public institutions is among several others an illustrious proof. That increase of all and especially of *sacred* literature, for which every age becomes more and more conspicuous, and which cannot in this place without the highest ingratitude be passed over in silence; that knowledge of God, of his works, and of his laws, which a *Christian* of a moderate capacity and reflection has in a degree greatly superior to the deepest *philosopher* of *paganism*, are a happy prelude and pledge of those more enlightened ed days, when *ᵂ the earth shall be full of the knowledge of the Lord as the waters cover the sea; ˣ for they shall know me from the least of them unto the greatest of them, saith the Lord.*

Who does not feel a conscious dignity and a laudable ambition of proceeding *ʸ from strength to strength, ᶻ from glory to glory,* at the very idea of that high excellence with which the nature he partakes of will be ennobled? If however any should, upon the reflection of his own personal inferiority, find humiliating and mortifying thoughts arise; let him compare his condition with that of those who lived in former ages; of those who are not yet enlightened by *ᵃ the sun of righteousness,* who even now *ᵇ sit in darkness and in the shadow of death,* and he will find abundant matter of consolation, joy, and triumph: let him re-

ᵂ *Is.* xi. 9.   ˣ *Jer.* xxxi. 34.
ʸ *Ps.* lxxxiv. 7.   ᶻ 2 *Cor.* iii. 18.
ᵃ *Mal.* iv. 2.   ᵇ *Luke* i. 79.

collect

collect that as ^c God adapts his revelations to the capacities of mankind in general, so likewise does he his demands to the abilities of individuals; that, if he has not granted him perfection, he will not exact perfection; that, provided his intention is upright and his obedience sincere, his great creator will through the powerful merits and intercession of his redeemer overlook his defects, pardon his failings, and by the preventing, strengthening, and sanctifying grace of his holy spirit enable him to perform an acceptable duty. If he does not in this world converse with those only *^d which are written in the lamb's book of life*; if he feels anxiety, pain, sickness and other harbingers of his approaching dissolution, let him remember that to a true Christian death is a passage unto life, *^e unto the city of the living God, the heavenly Jerusalem, and to an innu-*

^c Σύμμιῆρα ταῖς ἡλικίαις προσφέρει παιδεύμαῖα ὁ Θεὸς. *Theodor. har. fab.* l. v. c. 11.

^d *Rev.* xxi. 27.   ^e *Heb.* xii. 22, 23, 24.

merable

merable company of angels, to the general assembly and church of the first born which are written in heaven, and to God the judge of all, and to the spirits of just men made perfect, and to Jesus the mediator of the new covenant.

SERMON IV.

Ephes. i. 3.

Blessed be God and the father of our Lord Jesus Christ, who hath blessed us with all spiritual blessings in heavenly places in Christ.

A *Seeming* or *real* obscurity in the original has given occasion to several different interpretations of the latter part of this passage. The words, in the explaining of which learned men disagree, are ἐν τοῖς ἐπυρανίοις Χριστῶ, expressed in our version by *in heavenly places in Christ*. Some by the words τοῖς ἐπουρανίοις understand heavenly *things* not *places*;

meaning

meaning either the supernatural gifts then imparted to the church, or that state of immortality in heaven to which we hope to be exalted through *Christ*. But this exposition makes no distinction between this word and the εὐλογία πνευματικῇ *spiritual blessings* just before mentioned. Besides the Apostle constantly uses the word to signify heavenly *places* not *things*; and in this very epistle in three different passages, where the context unquestionably confines it to this sense. Thus in the *twentieth* verse of *this* chapter, *he raised him from the dead and set him at his own right hand* ἐν τοῖς ἐπουρανίοις *in heavenly places*; and in the *sixth* verse of the *next* chapter, *hath raised us together and made us sit together* ἐν τοῖς ἐπουρανίοις *in heavenly places*; and in the *tenth* verse of the *third* chapter, *to the intent that now to the principalities and powers* ἐν τοῖς ἐπουρανίοις "*in heavenly places*" *might be known by the church the manifold wisdom of God.* And this observation will lead us to the true meaning of a parallel expression in the *eighteenth* verse of *this* chapter—*the eyes of your understanding being enlightened that ye may know what is the*

the hope of his calling, and what the riches of the glory of his inheritance ἐν τοῖς ἁγίοις not *in the saints*, as our version has it, but *in the holy places*, i. e. how glorious an inheritance is purchased for us in heaven. But to return—There are who make the words *in Christ* to be emphatical and expressive of that *gathering together* (as it is called in verse the tenth) compacting and uniting together all people, Jews and Gentiles *in him*, in one church of which he is the head. [a] Others again think that the dative Χριστῷ is put instead of the genitive Χριστοῦ by an ellipsis of the participle οὖσι, making the words τοῖς ἐπουρανίοις Χριστῷ equivalent to τοῖς ἐπουρανίοις τοῖς οὖσι Χριστῷ heavenly things *of Christ* or *belonging unto Christ*.

All these Interpretations contain found truth, but do not seem to me to express the Apostles meaning. The passage indeed I take to be elliptical; but I think that the ellipsis should be supplied not with

---

[a] *Raphelius* seems to adopt this opinion, and brings authorities for it; but I do not think that any of his examples are fully to the point.

οὖσι

ἐῶσι but οὔκι. *Blessed be God and the father of our Lord Jesus Christ, who hath blessed us with all spiritual blessings through Christ* ἐν τοῖς ἐπουρανίοις οὔκι *after,* or, *in consequence of his ascension into heaven.* Whilst he was on earth *the holy spirit* (as we are told by [b] St. *John) was not yet, because Jesus was not yet glorified.* But when, upon his ascension and session at the right hand of God, he took the full and complete exercise of the offices consequent upon his mediatorial kingdom, he then by his ministry and intercession obtained whatever was necessary for the comfort, instruction, and support of his church. [c] *Being exalted to the right hand of God* (says St. *Peter* on the day of *Pentecost) and having received of the father the promise of the Holy Ghost, he hath shed forth this which you now see and hear.* This had been predicted by the royal prophet. [d] *Thou hast ascended on high; thou hast led captivity captive; thou hast received gifts for men.* And this prophecy our Apostle in this very

[b] *John* vii. 39. [c] *Acts* ii. 33.
[d] *Ps.* lxviii. 18.

epistle

SERMON IV.   123

epistle applies to the gracious dispensation of the holy spirit after our Lord's triumphant ascension, which it is observable that he mentions as of necessity preceding the grant of spiritual gifts,---*he ascended up far above all heavens that he might fill all things.*

These blessed effects of *Christ*'s glorification are by our Apostle in one place called *the first fruits of the spirit*, in another *the earnest of the spirit*, and in this chapter more emphatically still *the earnest of our inheritance*. Now these terms *first fruits* and *earnest* plainly intimate that the divine communications and comforts of the spirit, with which sincere Christians are favoured in this world, are in their nature similar, however inferior in degree, to those that shall hereafter constitute our happiness in heaven. As there is a twofold redemption, so is there likewise a twofold beatitude: the *first* redemption, consisting of absolution from the guilt and

e *Ephes.* iv. 10.   f *Rom.* viii. 23.
g 2 *Cor.* i. 22.   h V. 14.

condem-

condemnation of past sins, we enjoy in this life; the second, being an advancement to a state of incorruption and immortality, we expect through faith and hope. The sanctification of our minds, being in the best of us here on earth only initial and incomplete, is attended with only an initial and incomplete happiness; yet are they both a preparation for, a tendency unto, a prelude and foretaste of their completion and perfection. They are, says St. *Paul, an* [i] *earnest of our inheritance until the purchased possession,* i. e. until the *second redemption,* when we shall be put in possession of the inheritance purchased for us.

Twice did God by a voice from heaven testify that our blessed Saviour was his beloved son; at his [k] *baptism* and [l] *transfiguration*; an unanswerable argument against the *Socinians* who presume to assert that he was first made the son of God by his resurrection. But the reason of my making

---

[i] *Ephes.* i. 14. [k] *Matth.* iii. 17. *Mark* i. 11.
[l] *Matth.* xvii. 5. *Mark* ix. 7. *Luke* ix. 35.

the obfervation at prefent is, becaufe the occafion of this twofold fupernatural declaration of the dignity of our redeemer, feems to me to have a refpect to the diftinction I have, after others, made of a twofold redemption; the firft occafion was his *baptifm*, when he was inaugurated into his prophetical office, and began to preach the *firft redemption, remiffion of fins:* the fecond occafion of this divine teftimony, was his *transfiguration,* when he was pleafed to give three of his difciples a glimpfe and pledge of that fplendor, with which ᵐ *our vile bodies* fhall be invefted when they are *fafhioned like unto his glorious body:* i. e. at the *fecond redemption,* when we fhall be releafed not only from the guilt but from the punifhment of fin; for fin fhall be left buried in the grave, and the foul being purged and perfected fhall be joined to the body fpiritualized and fitted for a celeftial ftate; and both together enjoy eternal life.

With thefe *fpiritual bleffings,* the com-

ᵐ *Phil.* iii. 21.

pletion of all blessings, *has God* more particularly *blessed us in consequence of Christ's ascension into heaven.* It is the exemplary assimilative cause of ours. As he died and rose again for us, that [n] *we, by dying unto sin, might be planted together in the likeness of his death,* and by henceforth living unto God, *in the likeness of his resurrection;* so was he glorified that [o] *we also might be glorified together,* On the day of his ascension he took possession of heaven for us [p] *that where he is we might be also.* [q] *He is entered as our fore-runner,* as the representative of his church and people: for as the *natural* so likewise the *mystical* body is partaker of all the honours of its head: his advancement is the advancement of us all, his ascension the surety of ours; and therefore St. *Paul* to denote in the strongest manner their inseparable connexion triumphantly joins them together, and speaks of *our* exaltation as a thing already accomplished in consequence and virtue of

---

[n] *Rom.* vi. 5.   [o] *Rom.* viii. 17.
[p] *John* xiv. 3.
[q] *Heb.* vi. 20. ἔνθεν ἡ κεφαλὴ, ἐκεῖ κȷ τὸ σῶμα· οὐδενὶ μέσῳ διείργεται ἡ κεφαλὴ κȷ τὸ σῶμα. *Chrys. in Eph.* λ. 3.

the

the exaltation of *Christ*; ^r *he* hath *quickened us together with Christ, and* hath *raised us up together and* made *us fit together in heavenly places through Christ Jesus.*

To render the true and full understanding of this doctrine more easy and familiar, it may not be amiss to take a short view of that institution which was typical and figurative of it; and which our great Apostle in his sublime epistle to the *Hebrews* constantly appeals to as explanatory of this great mystery: and this I shall do the more willingly, because it will at the same time illustrate and confirm that main article of the Christian faith, that great source and original of all Christian privileges—the vicarious punishment of *Christ* and the piacular virtue of his blood.

We are told by St. *Peter* that ^s *the prophets— enquired and searched diligently what or what manner of time the spirit of Christ which was in them did signify.* By the *prophets* here are in an enlarged and compre-

^r *Ephes.* ii. 5, 6.   ^s 1 *Pet.* i. 10, 11.

hensive

henfive fenfe meant all the *faithful* from the beginning of the world, to whom the bleffing of the *Meſſiah* was promifed or revealed; all the *patriarchs* who [t] *having seen the promiſes afar off were perſuaded of them and embraced them*; all the true *Iſraelites* who may without impropriety be faid to have believed in *Chriſt* even before his coming: And this I verily believe to be our Apoſtle's meaning when he tells the *Epheſians* that the Jews were [u] προηλπικότες ἐν τῷ Χριςῷ; which words, taken according to this their plain and original import, ſtrongly mark a diſtinction made between the Jews and the Gentiles; which diſtinction is entirely loſt in our and other verſions—" [w] *that we ſhould be to the praiſe of his glory*"—" we *(Jews)*

---

[t] *Heb.* xi. 13.

[u] Προελπίζειν dici poſſunt, et qui prius quam alii ſperant, et qui ſpem de aliquâ re præcipiunt. Priorem ſententiam defendit *Beza* tanquam ſolam veram, alteram prorſus rejiciens quæ *Ambroſii* eſt, ſtatuentis Apoſtolos in *judaiſmo* quoque verſantes tamen ſpem habuiſſe in *Chriſto* venturo, utpote quem ex prophetarum oraculis expectarint. Diſtinguit enim *Paulus* Judæos a Gentilibus hoc diſcrimine, quod illi in *Chriſto* etiam venturo ſpem poſuerint, hi vero ante evangelium fuerint ſine *Chriſto*, ut infra 2. 12. dicit; ἤτε ἐν τῷ καιρῷ ὀκείνω χωρὶς Χριςῦ. *Raphel. in loc.*

[w] *Epheſ.* i. 12.

who

"who hoped in Chrift *before* his coming;" in whom " ye *(Gentiles)* alfo hoped *after* that ye heard the word of truth, the gofpel of falvation." The *Jews* did hope in *Chrift before* his coming. [x] *For the hope of Ifrael,* fays St. Paul fpeaking to them, *I am bound with this chain:* And to [y] *Agrippa,* (a prince *expert in all cuftoms and queftions which were among the Jews) now I ftand and am judged for the hope of the promife made of God unto our fathers; unto which promife our twelve tribes inftantly ferving God day and night hope to come.*

God, having from the beginning of time conceived in his eternal mind the idea of the redemption, gave fallen man continual notices of it, reprefenting it under different figures and emblems; beyond which and through which the believers of old, according to the meafure of revelation granted them, looked forwards to their fubftance, and firmly relying on the veracity of God [z] *obtained a*

[x] *Acts* xxviii. 20.   [y] *Acts* xxvi. 3. 6, 7.
[z] *Heb.* xi. 39.

I   good

good report through faith though they received not the promise. If they therefore, in those days of uncertainty, directed their minds through the obscurity of present shadows towards the light to come; surely a Christian, on whom that light shines in full glory, must find a singular pleasure in throwing back his eye upon those models and portraitures of his salvation; the exact likeness of which in every minute circumstance must convince him that they were sketched out by the hand of God himself; that both the shadow and substance, the type and antitype, proceeded from him who is [a]*Alpha and Omega, the beginning and the end, the first and the last.*

The first emblematical notice given of a future redemption, was undoubtedly by the institution of sacrifices; [b] which method of worship, whatever is asserted by

---

[a] *Revel.* xxii. 13.

[b] See among others *Shuckford.* V. 1. One would think, says bishop *Patrick* on *Genes.* iv. 3. that *Plato* had some notion of this, when he forbids his lawgiver (in his *Epinomis*) to make any alteration in the rites of sacrificing, because οὐ δυνατὸν εἰδέναι τῇ θνητῇ ᾗ τοιούτων πέρι *it is not possible for our mortal nature to know any thing about such matters.*

men

men strangely averse to any interposition of the deity, has surely no foundation in nature, and therefore must have been suggested by divine revelation. It is probable, from the use we find made of them upon God's future treating with mankind, that he was at their first institution pleased to enter into a covenant with man, of which a sacrifice was the seal and ratification. That there were conditions, which are a necessary part of a covenant, required of man; and that one principal condition was *faith* can admit of no doubt; for St. *Paul*, speaking of the first sacrifice upon record, expresly says, that ^c *by* faith *Abel offered a more excellent sacrifice than Cain.* Now what is *faith* but a firm reliance on the promises of God? and what had God promised but a *redeemer?* Thus therefore were sacrifices not only typical representations of the sacrifice of the promised redeemer, whose blood was to be the seal of a new covenant; but moreover God's acceptance of them was a sacramental sign and pledge of his reconcilia-

---

^c *Heb.* xi. 4.

tion to man through *faith* in him, the anticipating and retroactive virtue of whose blood would extend the benefits of salvation through all ages. [d] *If thou doest well*, says God to *Cain*, i. e. if thou offerest thy sacrifice from a true principle, *shalt thou not be accepted? And if thou doest not well, sin lieth at the door*, i. e. thy sacrifice shall not make atonement for thy sin.

This practice of substituting an innocent animal in the room of the offender, was religiously transmitted by *Noah* after the flood to all his descendents, and observed universally by all nations, however they differed in other religious rites. But its divine origin and typical design being together with the other parts of patriarchal worship forgotten, God was pleased to separate a peculiar people for the preservation of true religion and faith in the promised saviour. With them he made a new covenant ratifying it with the usual seal of sacrifice, which he again expressly

[d] *Genes.* iv. 7.

enjoined

enjoined with such additional circumstances and ceremonies, [e] as plainly denoted its expiatory quality and typical relation to that grand atonement, of which it was intended to keep up a memorial.

I might here run a parallel, which would be found to correspond with the minutest exactness, between all the particulars attending the legal sacrifices and that of our blessed Saviour: but, as those offered on the great day of atonement had a more especial regard to it, I shall content myself with considering a few of the ceremonies then used; which I hope will sufficiently explain and fully confirm the doctrines I have just now advanced.

[f] *Aaron* (says God himself) *shall lay both his hands upon the live goat, and confess over him all the iniquities of the children of Israel and all their transgressions in all their sins, putting them upon the head of the goat.*

---

[e] See *Outram de Sacrificiis*, l. i. c. 18. and *Berriman*'s *Sermons at Boyle*'s *Lectures*.
[f] *Levit.* xvi. 21.

This form of imposition of hands and confession of sins was used in all sacrifices, and is very expressive of transferring the sins confessed upon the victim, and devoting it to bear the punishment of them. Upon all other occasions the victim thus loaded with guilt was brought to the altar, and slain instead of the offender: but on this more solemn occasion two goats made up but one sin-offering: one of them was offered in sacrifice, the other was sent away alive; by the first was represented our Saviour's being [s] *delivered* to death *for our offences*, by the second his being *raised again for our justification*.

On that day only did the high-priest, and none but him, enter into the holy of holies burning incense; and, having dipped his fingers in the blood of the several victims offered, he sprinkled it towards the mercy seat, and pronounced a solemn blessing on the people uttering on that occasion and no other the peculiar and incommunicable name of God. We may

[s] Rom. iv. 25.

here

here first observe, that it was not till after the expiation of himself, as well as of the priests and people, that the high-priest presumed to enter into the most holy place: for there is an inseparable connection between holiness and glory; to set which in the strongest light *Christ* himself, our great *high-priest* (though he had even during his stay upon earth an absolute inherent holiness, yet as he had taken our sins upon himself, even he) could not, loaded as he was though with imputed impurities, enter into the true holy of holies, till he had made that full and perfect satisfaction for them, which as our surety he had undertaken to make, to the justice of God: but a compleat atonement being made, and [h] *sin put away by the sacrifice of himself he entered, not into the holy places made with hands which are the figures of the true, but into heaven itself now to appear in the presence of God for us.*

The incense offered, and the blood sprinkled, were undoubtedly symbols of

[h] *Heb.* ix. 26.

Christ's presenting himself with his blood in the heavens, exhibiting in the presence of God the merits of his sufferings, and together with them [i] *offering up* (as the *Angel of the covenant* is represented to do in the *Revelations) the prayers of the saints*, rendering them acceptable to God through his own efficacious mediation and intercession.

After the legal high-priest had gone through all these symbolical ceremonies, he pronounced the solemn blessing.— [k] JEHOVAH *bless thee and keep thee.* JEHOVAH *make his face to shine upon thee and be gracious unto thee.* JEHOVAH *lift up his countenance upon thee and give thee peace.* Whatever mystery may be contained in

---

[i] *Revel.* viii. 3.
[k] *Numb.* vi. 24, 25, 26. Maximè μυστηριώδης est *trina nominis Jehovæ repetitio. Prima pericopa* percommode refertur ad *Patrem,* de quo *Paulus* scribit. *Ephes.* i. 3. *Deus et* PATER—*qui* BENEDIXIT *nobis omni spirituali benedictione in Christo,* et cui *Christus* ipse dicit. *Joh.* xvii. 11. SERVA *eos per nomen tuum. Altera pericopa ad* CHRISTUM pertinet qui est *Lux mundi. Joh.* viii. 12. *Ultima pericopa,* cum notet applicationem gratiæ, et communicationem pacis ac gaudii, commode applicatur SPIRITUI SANCTO *per quem regnum Dei nobis est justitia et pax et gaudium. Rom.* xiv. 17. *Witsius de Sacerdotio Aaronis et Christi.*

the

the ufe, upon that particular day, and the trinal repetition of this facred name, as was fufpected by the Jews themfelves; this however is very evident, that the atonement was not compleated, nor the people entitled to the bleffings to be conferred in confequence of it, till the blood of the victim was prefented before the mercy feat. And herein is fhadowed forth by a very appofite emblem the full and ultimate accomplifhment of the reconciliation obtained by the great expiatory facrifice for the fins of the whole world.

[l] *The Tabernacle, fay the Jews, is a book of wifdom to inftruct men in the things above.* The adytum, or holy of holies, fays [m] *Jofephus, which was inaccefſible to the prieſts, reprefented heaven where God dwelt.* And this interpretation is undoubtedly right. For, as the Apoftle argues, [n] *the way into the holieſt of all was not yet made manifeſt while as the firſt tabernacle was yet ſtanding: but our high-prieſt having*

[l] Buxt. hiſt. arc. [m] Jof. ant. l. iii. c. vi. 4.
[n] Heb. x. 20.

confecrated

consecrated a new way for us the veil is rent, and heaven rendered accessible to all believers. ° His sacrifice of himself was indeed offered in this earthly tabernacle; but his sacerdotal office was not fully discharged, till he had, by the presentation of his blood, testified that the atonement was actually made and ᴾ *the holy place reconciled.* Then were the ᑫ *everlasting doors* of heaven opened, and together with *the king of glory* did every faithful believer even then virtually enter.

But while we thus contend that heaven was rendered accessible at our Lord's ascension, let us not forget to ascribe this blessing in point of *efficient causality* to his

---

° Pontifex Judæorum et pontifex noster *Jesus Christus*; sanguis hircorum et vitulorum (eorum utique qui diebus *expiationis* mactabantur) et sanguis *Christi*; intimum adytum, et cœlum supremum; ac denique pontificis in adytum illud ingressus per victimarum earum sanguinem, et ingressus *Christi* in cælum ipsum sui ipsius sanguinis vi; ut res adumbrantes et adumbratæ inter se mutuò conferuntur. *Outram.* l. i. c. 18.

ᴾ *Levit.* xvi. 20.

ᑫ *Ps.* xxiv. 7. Ὅτι ἐκ νεκρῶν ἀνέστη καὶ ἀνέβαινεν εἰς τ̀ οὐρανὸν, κελευόντων οἱ ἐν τοῖς οὐρανοῖς ταχθέντες ὑπὸ τ̀ Θεῦ ἄρχοντες ἀνοῖξαι τὰς πύλας τ̀ οὐρανῶν —*Justin Mart.* speaking of our Saviour's *resurrection* and *ascension. Dial. cum Tryph.* p. 107.

oblation

SERMON IV.   139

oblation upon the crofs; of which his oblation in heaven was the proof, the evidence, the credential. He thereby (to fpeak after the manner of men) produced his title-deed, and took poffeffion of the purchafed inheritance. The price he paid for it was his blood. He was not only our *prieſt* but our *ſacrifice*. ' *Chriſt loved us and gave himſelf for us an offering and a* ſacrifice *to God.* He was not only our *propitiator* but our *propitiation.* ' *God loved us and ſent his ſon to be the* propitiation *for our ſins.* He was not only our *redeemer* but our *ranſom.* ' *He gave himſelf* a ranſom *for all.* Now ſince by the Jewiſh law, from which theſe expreſſions are taken, the ſins of the offender were always transferred upon the *ſacrifice*; ſince the ſacrifice thus ſuffering inſtead of the offender was called the *propitiation*; ſince the conſideration paid to reſcue the firſt-born from death was called the *ranſom*—what can the Apoſtles mean, when they tell us that *Chriſt* was our *ſacrifice, propitiation, and*

' *Epheſ.* v. 2.   ' 1 *John* iv. 10.
    ' 1 *Tim.* ii. 6.

ranſom,

ranſom, but that *our* ſins *were transferred upon him,* that *he ſuffered in our ſtead,* and that *his ſuffering reſcued us from death?* Every text in holy writ, which ſpeaks of our redemption, confirms this doctrine. ᵘ *He redeemed us from the curſe being made a curſe for us,* ʷ *he was made ſin for us,* not that he contracted any guilt, but having taken our ſins upon him he underwent the puniſhment of them, ˣ which puniſhment the law ſtiled accurſed. We ʸ *were not redeemed with corruptible things, but with the precious blood of Chriſt:* for ᶻ *him hath God ſet forth,* (not, as the followers of *Socinus* impiouſly aſſert, merely as an example of holy life, and to confirm by his death the truth of his doctrine, but) *to be a propitiation though faith in his blood.*

The death of our Saviour was undoubtedly a full and authentic confirmation of the truth of the goſpel, and hence it is called by St. *Paul,* ᵃ *a good confeſſion:* but this end could not ſurely be the only one

---

ᵘ *Galat.* iii. 13.
ˣ *Deuter.* xxi. 23.
ᶻ *Rom.* iii. 25.
ʷ 2 *Cor.* v. 21.
ʸ 1 *Pet.* i. 18, 19.
ᵃ 1 *Tim.* vi. 13.

designed; there must have been some more cogent reason to induce God to permit the son of his bosom to undergo a cruel and ignominious death. The truth of the gospel was abundantly evinced by the miracles he performed, and the testimony of all the prophets since the world began. If these proofs were not sufficient, [b] would not however a display of his power by a miraculous descent from the cross have been a more illustrious confirmation, than submitting to the torments and shame of punishment? If *Christ* was only set forth as an example, what need was there of his death? was not his doctrine a sufficient rule of life? was not the whole tenor of his life instructive and exemplary, a perfect pattern of patience, meekness, courage, charity, purity, holiness, and every virtue that constitutes innocence? The blood of martyrs shed in the cause of religion bore testimony to the truth, and they have both in their lives and death set us eminent examples of con-

---

[b] *If he be the king of Israel*, said the chief priests with the scribes and elders, *let him now come down from the cross, and we will believe him.* Matth. xxvii. 41, 42.

stancy,

stancy, humility, and other christian virtues. Yet in what part of scripture are we taught that their blood was shed for us, or that we should build our faith upon them? St. *Paul* reprobates the idea with the highest indignation. *Was Paul crucified for you? or were you baptized in the name of Paul?* *who then is Paul and who is Apollos but ministers? for other foundation can no man lay than that is laid, which is Jesus Christ.*

The death of our blessed Saviour, taken abstractedly from every other consideration, does not seem to have any thing in it peculiar or extraordinary: many holy men had before him, many holy men have since, suffered as cruel and bloody a death. If there was therefore no mystery in his death and passion, why are they so celebrated and magnified in the holy scriptures? If there was no singular and specific virtue in his blood, why is there such an emphasis laid upon it throughout the whole word of God? Surely there must

---

c 1 *Cor.* i. 13.   d 1 *Cor.* iii. 5. 11.

have

have been something peculiar in the ᵉ nature and design of his sufferings, which distinguished them from all other sufferings; some secret quality in his blood, to occasion such peculiar notice, such particular marks and characters to accompany constantly the mention and description of it. Why did our Saviour himself with so much solemnity institute and recommend the sacrament, as a memorial of his body broken and blood shed? Why are there promises of such extraordinary blessings annexed to the worthy participation of the *sacramental*, if there was no extraordinary virtue, no important mystery in the *real* flesh and blood, whereof the one was broken the other shed upon the cross?

The scriptures explain this mystery; there we are taught that his sufferings were *vicarious*, his blood *piacular*; ᶠ *he washed us from our sins in his own blood*, ᵍ *he*

ᵉ Very expressive is that ejaculation in the *greek* liturgies Διὰ τ̅ ἀγνώστων σου παθημάτων ἐλέησον ἡμᾶς, Χριστέ: *By thy* unknown *sufferings, O Christ have mercy upon us.*

ᶠ *Revel.* i. 5.   ᵍ *Ibid.* v. 9.

redeemed

redeemed us to God by his blood: [h] *he was wounded for our transgressions; he was bruised for our iniquities; the chastisement of our peace was upon him, and with his stripes are we healed; all we like sheep had gone astray, and the Lord hath laid upon him the iniquities of us all.* Of these iniquities his death was piacular; for them he underwent the accumulated wrath, and satisfied the infinite justice of God. Hence he is said [i] *his own self to have born our sins in his own body on the tree,* [k] *to have given himself for our sins,* [l] *to have died for our sins.* And, to make us more easily apprehend this mystery, he is compared to the *propitiatory sacrifices* under the law, which were always understood [m] *to make atonement* for the sins of him who offered them. Now this virtue of theirs reason and the nature of things must teach us could only be symbolical: for, as St. *Paul* justly argues, [n] *it is not possible that the blood of bulls and*

---

[h] *If.* liii. 5.
[k] *Galat.* i. 4.
[m] *Levit.* i. 4.
[i] 1 *Pet.* ii. 24.
[l] 1 *Cor.* xv. 3.
[n] *Heb.* x. 4. Even our learned *Spencer* himself, who is so strenuous an advocate for the *human institution* of sacrifices, is forced to acknowledge that *humanæ menti, naturæ divinæ*

SERMON IV.

of goats could take away fins. If this is true, and it is moft evidently fo, how could reafon prompt man to make ufe of a method for the expiation of his fins, which that very reafon muft affure him was of itfelf inadequate to the effect? But the effect itfelf was likewife fymbolical. The deliverance they effected was only from *temporal* death; and the privileges they obtained were merely *ceremonial*, the right of joining in the public worfhip and approaching the fanctuary. But, as they had a refpect to the facrifice of *Chrift* their antitype and fubftance, they from that relation acquired a degree of fuperior excellence: the legal purity, the admiffion to

---

divinæ fcientiâ vel leviter imbutæ, manifeftum eft facrificio per fe fpectato nihil ineffe, unde ullo apud Deum in pretio effe poffet. Nothing, I think, can be plainer than that God appointed *Animals* to be offered as figures and reprefentations of the facrifice of the Meffiah, whofe *blood* was to atone for the fins of the whole world. And hence the reafon why *unto Cain and his offering God had not refpect. Genef.* iv. 5. His *offering* was of the fruit of the ground, *bloodlefs*; and therefore could not be accepted: for *without blood there can be no redemption. Heb.* ix. 22. Neither therefore could *Cain* himfelf be accepted; for not having *faith* in the promifes of God he brought a different offering from that which he had appointed; an offering which, having no typical relation to the one great offering, could not entitle him to the benefits annexed to thofe only that had that relation.

K   the

the holy place, and deliverance from temporal death, became reprefentatives of the *fpiritual* purity, the accefs unto God, and the title to *eternal* life purchafed for us by the precious blood of *Chrift*. °*For if the blood of bulls and of goats—fanctifieth to the purifying of the flefh, how much more fhall the blood of Chrift purge the confcience?*

Though I have already taken up fo much of your time, I muft ftill beg your patience and attention to an inference or two; whofe great importance, and clofe connection with the doctrine I have endeavoured to confirm, will not fuffer me entirely to neglect and pafs them over in filence.

It is evident, from moft of the paffages which I have cited, that the *redemption* wrought by the blood of *Chrift* is *univerfal*. It is the conftant and uniform language of fcripture; and yet it cannot be true if, according to the *Socinians*, *Chrift* was fet forth only as a teacher of truth

---

° *Heb.* ix. 13, 14.

and an example of holiness; for then he could have no retrospect to past generations; that truth could be professed, and that example followed, by those only to whom they were proposed. But, what comfort could our first parents reap from a promise of a redeemer, if they were to have no benefit from the redemption? The promise was universal, and therefore they to whom it was made must certainly be included in it. Every subsequent covenant established with the patriarchs was a renewal of it: And hence St. *Paul* says that [p] *God preached the gospel to Abraham, saying, In thy seed shall all nations be blessed;* and it was faith in this promise that [q] *was counted unto him for righteousness:* the same faith made [r] *Moses esteem the reproach of Christ greater riches than the treasures of Egypt;* and this faith entitled him, and every true believer, to *the recompence of the reward.* Either sacrifices were sufficient to satisfy the justice of God, or they were not: if they were sufficient, there needed

---

[p] *Galat.* iii. 8.   [q] *Rom.* iv. 3.
[r] *Heb.* xi. 26.

no redeemer; if they were not, the efficacy of *his* blood muſt be reflected back upon thoſe who offered them. And upon this is founded the Apoſtle's argument, that if *Chriſt*'s once offering himſelf had not been effectual ˢ *he muſt often have ſuffered ſince the foundation of the world.* But ᵗ *Jeſus Chriſt is the ſame yeſterday, to day, and for ever.* The efficacy of his ſacrifice extends through all ages from the beginning to the end of the world.

As the benefits of *Chriſt*'s paſſion are univerſal with regard to *time* ſo are they likewiſe with regard to *perſons*. He died for all without exception, without diſtinction. The words made uſe of in ſcripture are plain, familiar, and explicit, teaching us that all mankind univerſally are the ſubject of redemption. ᵘ *Chriſt gave him-*

ˢ *Heb.* ix. 26.   ᵗ *Heb.* xiii. 8.
ᵘ *Tim.* ii. 4 6. It is obſervable that the common Syriac and Dr. *Ridley*'s old MS. ſeem both of them to have read ὑπὲρ παντὸς inſtead of πάντων, *he gave himſelf a ranſom for every individual man.* The Verſion, ſays the Doctor, may rather be a proof of a Syriac Idiom than a various reading in the original; however it proves their ſenſe of the paſſage that *the ranſom was for every individual, and not for ſome only of every kind.*

ſelf

self a ransom for all; he will have all men to be saved; ^w *he is the lamb of God that taketh away the sins of the world,* ^x *the propitiation for the sins of the* whole *world*. As those who were redeemed are *collectively* expressed by the words *all, the world,* and *the whole world,* so likewise are they *dis- tributively*. ^y *The Lord is not willing that any should perish;* ^z *he tasted death* ὑπὲρ παντὸς *for* every individual *man*. The universality of the redemption is plainly taught in the parallel, which the Apostle draws between the effects of *Adam's disobedience* and those of *the obedience of Christ.* ^a *As by the offence of one judgement came upon* all men *to condemnation, so by the righteousness of one the free gift came upon* all men *unto justification of life:* ^b *As in Adam* all *die, so in Christ shall* all *be made alive.* ^c The whole Chris-

---

^w *John* i. 29.   ^x 1 *John* ii. 2.
^y 2 *Pet.* iii. 9.   ^z *Heb.* ii. 9.
^a *Rom.* v. 18.   ^b 1 *Cor.* xv. 22.

^c Persuasio nostra non est ex eo qui vocavit nos, sed ex nobis qui consentimus vocanti: aliud quippe dei opus, aliud hominum; dei opus est vocare, hominum credere vel non credere.—Accusat enim quare non obediverint veritati, ostendens in eorum arbitrio positum obedire vel non obedire. *Hier. in Galat.* v. 8. In this he speaks the sense of all the ancients till St. *Austin's* time. *Whitby.* This point is very fully and ably treated by the late learned Dr. *Ridley*

tian church for the first four hundred years maintained this comfortable truth; all the Christian writers during that period uniformly agree in this doctrine; ascribing the condemnation of men, not to any *partial purpose or irrespective decree* of God but to their own free choice, not to *his denial* of grace but to *their neglect* of it when proffered. St. *Austin* first broached the contrary doctrine of *election and reprobation*, falling (it is to be hoped inadvertently) in the warmth of a dispute against *Pelagius*, whose tenets were subversive of *universal*, into the opposite extreme of *particular* and *irresistible* grace. The credit however which he gained in this controversy was so great, that his writings became the foundation on which the latin fathers and schoolmen erected their theology; they were prescribed by the authority of the Popes as a rule never to be swerved from in all schools and universities. Hence this rigid doctrine became so rooted in the church that even the first reformers,

---

Ridley in his Sermons at Lady Moyer's lectures, to which I beg leave to refer the reader.

though

though in general men of learning, piety, and judgement yet (being according to the custom of the times particularly versed in his writings, and impressed with an invincible notion of his superior excellence) blindly professed, and strenuously maintained it, without examining its beginning or progress. But when the study of the holy scriptures and the more ancient fathers came into repute and use, the authority of St. *Austin* (^d which in truth was challenged in support of doctrines much more extravagant than those which he really taught) gave way to the uniform opinion of the catholic church in early ages, to the reason of man, to the word of God. They would in all probability have died had it not been for their subserviency to the designs of artful sectaries, who have of late years not only embraced but ^e im-

---

^d There are several passages in his writings, which give room to suppose that his real opinion is not to be gathered from those unguarded expressions, leaning too much to *Manichæism*, into which his zeal hurried him in his dispute with *Pelagius*. Such is the following. *Vult Deus omnes homines salvos fieri, et in agnitionem veritatis venire a non sic tamen, ut eis adimat liberum arbitrium, quo vel bene vel male utentes justissime judicentur. Aug. ad Marc. de spir. et lit.* c. 33.

^e " Though all the sins that ever were committed in the
" whole

proved upon them, in spite of their anti-scriptural principle, and the horrid consequences with which they are justly chargeable. I tremble to mention the distinction made by *Thomas Aquinas*, and espoused by *Calvin* and his followers, of an *hidden* and *revealed* will of God contrary to each other. It reflects upon the veracity and goodness of God; it robs him of all his moral attributes, which endear him to his rational creatures; it makes his dealings with men fraudulent and illusive, in inviting them to a salvation which was never designed for them; in setting forth unto them a redeemer, in whom they really have no interest nor concern; in offering terms of reconciliation, which he is determined never to grant; in publishing pardon to all true penitents and believers, when he has secretly resolved that they shall not truly repent and believe, or if they do, yet they shall not partake of the pardon promised.

"whole world were centered in one soul, it would be no bar to its salvation." *Whitfield* and *Cummins*, as quoted by Dr. *Ridley*.

But

SERMON IV. 153

But let us turn away from this shocking scene though to one perhaps not much less shocking.

We have seen, from many plain and exprefs texts of fcripture, that *Chrift* died in our ftead, and that by his death he made an atonement and fatisfaction to the juftice of God for the fins of the whole world. Yet a neighbouring church, which infolently claims the title of catholic, in fact rejects that doctrine; it relies not on the fufferings or merits of our bleffed redeemer, from which the great pillars of that church tell us there comes no acceffion of dignity to the works of juft men, which ᶠ *do of themfelves by a value of condignity merit eternal life.* When thefe good works are wanting finners have recourfe not to the fatisfaction of *Chrift* but of *Saints,* with which they are abundantly fupplied out of a treafure pretended to be left to that church; to ᵍ *indulgences* and

---

ᶠ *Bellarm.* de juftific. l. v. c. 7.

ᵍ The novelty of *indulgences* and *pardons*, &c. is freely confeffed by many *Romifh* writers. Inter omnes res, de quibus in
hoc

pardons, which the Pope ufurps the power upon being paid properly of diftributing profufely. By thefe and various other methods of human inftitution do they feek for falvation ; " [h] methods derogatory "from the merits of our Saviour, contra-"dictory to common fenfe as well as "fcripture, which neither any Apoftles "ever taught, nor any fathers of the "church ever heard of."

We are told by St. *Paul* that *Chriſt, after he had offered one ſacrifice for ſins,* for ever *ſat down at the right hand of God,* and that *where there is remiſſion for ſins there is no more offering for ſin:* yet the church of Rome facrilegioufly prefumes to bring *Chriſt* down every day from the right hand of God, to *crucify afreſh the*

---

hoc opere difputamus, nulla eft quam minus aperte S. literæ prodiderunt et de qua minus vetufti fcriptores dixerint ; neque tamen hàc occafione contemnendæ funt—— nam de *tranſubſtantione panis in corpus Chriſti* rara eft in antiquis fcriptoribus mentio—de *purgatorio* fere nulla.—Quid ergo mirum fi ad hunc modum contigerit de *indulgentiis* ut apud prifcos nulla fit de eis mentio ? *Alphonſ. Caſtro de hær.* l. 8. *Tit. de Indulgentiis.*

[h] *Brevint on the Maſs.*

Lord

SERMON IV.

Lord of glory; " [i] changing *his institution of a sacrament* into *a sacrifice of their own,* the *sacramental communication* of the body and blood of *Christ to man* into a proper and *real offering* of the same body and blood *to God;*" and this the Council of Trent declares to be [k] *a true and proper sacrifice really propitiatory for the sins, punishments, satisfactions, and other necessities, both of the living and the dead.*

But we, my brethren, thanks be to God have not so learned *Christ.* We acknowledge with gratitude that [l] *the offering of Christ once made is a perfect redemption, propitiation, and satisfaction for all the sins of the whole world,* and that *there is none other satisfaction for sin but that alone:* We believe that the blood shed in this sacrifice is the seal of the new covenant, by which God is pleased through the merits of his beloved son to remit our

---

[i] *Brevint on the Mass.*

[k] *Sess.* xxii. *ch.* 2. There are no less than nine canons relating to the mass, all of them containing anti-scriptural doctrine; yet each of them pronounces a curse against those that disbelieve it.

[l] *Article* 31st.

sins,

fins, and receive all mankind without respect of persons into grace and favour; that to them, who truly and sincerely endeavour to fulfil the terms of the covenant, *Christ* will be ^m *made wisdom, and righteousness, and sanctification, and redemption*; their minds will be enlightened, their sins forgiven; the means of grace will be powerfully imparted to them, and their obedience finally crowned with eternal life.—And this God will be pleased to perform, not through any merits of our own, but through the merits and satisfaction of his Son our Saviour *Jesus Christ*.

^m 1 *Cor.* i. 30.

SERMON V.

JOHN i. 1, 2, 3.

That which was from the beginning, which we have heard, which we have seen with our eyes, which we have looked upon, and our hands have handled of the word of life (for the life was manifested, and we have seen it, and bear witness, and shew unto you that eternal life which was with the father and was manifested unto us.) That which we have seen and heard declare we unto yon.

THE redemption of mankind is so wonderful in itself and so important in its consequences, that the most minute circumstance relating to it is highly deserving

serving our most serious and attentive consideration: how much more then are we bound by indispensible duty to endeavour at attaining a right notion of those more material truths, which constitute its very essence and substance? With this view, (after having in the foregoing discourses to the best of my abilities vindicated the first principles of religion in general, and the truth of the Christian religion in particular,) I proceeded to explain that state of perdition from which we were redeemed, and the nature, benefits, and universality of that redemption; rescuing constantly what has appeared to me to be the truth, as delivered by *Christ* and his Apostles, from the hand of the enemy. With the same view I propose, God willing, to employ the present discourse in considering from his word, contained in the scriptures, the nature of that blessed person by whom our redemption was effected; and for that purpose have chosen these words of St. *John*; because they evidently contain and assert two fundamental doctrines of a true Christian's belief on this sublime and important subject,

the

SERMON V.

the *humanity* and *divinity* of *Christ*. His *humanity* is plainly asserted in these words —*that which we have heard—which we have seen with our eyes—which we have looked upon and our hands have handled—the life was manifested*—expressions which, being thus by way of confirmation crouded upon each other and appealing to several of the senses, give us the fullest assurance of the certainty and reality of *Christ*'s incarnation and manifestation in the flesh. And that this person, who thus assumed human nature, had a distinct, *pre-existent*, and more excellent being the Apostle teaches us by saying that he *was from the beginning*, by calling him *the word of life* —*the life—that eternal life which was with the father.*

The words themselves without any comment point out the occasion on which they were written, and the heresies they were meant to oppose. They are chiefly directed against the [a] first heresy that arose

---

[a] Apostolis adhuc in sæculo superstitibus, adhuc apud Judæam *Christi* sanguine recenti, *phantasma* Domini corpus asserebatur. *Hieron. adv. Lucif.* c. 8.

in the church; a strange, absurd, and blasphemous doctrine taught by *Simon Magus* and his [b] followers—that *Jesus Christ* did not *really* come in the flesh, but that his incarnation was only in appearance, *putativè* as the latin fathers called it, or as the greeks ἐν δοκήσει and ἐν φαντασίᾳ; whence we often read of them under the names of *docetæ* and *phantasiastæ*. [c] As they denied the *reality* of our Saviour's human body, so they consequently held all his actions and sufferings to have been equally ideal;

---

[b] They were called *gnostics* from the greek word γνῶσις: which in general signifies *knowledge*, but in the language of scripture is often used for a particular gift vouchsafed in the infancy of the church, the *knowledge of mysteries*: which gift these heretics pretending to have in a more especial manner assumed to themselves the name of γνωστικοὶ *gnostics*, i. e. *the men of knowledge*, as if they had been the only persons that understood and could expound the mysteries of the Christian faith. Thus the first temptation which *Satan* threw in the way of man in the state of *grace*, was the very same to which he had so easily yielded in the state of *nature*.

[c] Thus *Tertullian* speaking of one *Cerdon* a ring-leader among these heretics. Hunc *(Christum)* in substantiâ carnis negat, in *phantasmate* solo fuisse pronuntiat: nec omninò passum, sed *quasi* passum; nec ex virgine natum, sed omnino nec natum. de præsc. hæret. c. 51. *Basilides* (as we are told by *Philastrius* in his book *de hæres.*) added this peculiarity to the other absurdities that *Simon of Cyrene suffered* instead of our *Saviour*, because it is said in scripture *that he bore his cross*.

he

he was not *really* born of the Virgin *Mary*, neither did he *really* eat, drink, or sleep; he was not *really* crucified, neither did he *really* die or rise again: All these things were done only *in appearance, in a phantasm,* or *vision.*

It was, I am persuaded, with reference to this heresy that St. *John* began his first general epistle in the words of my text; it was with a particular view to it that he wrote both this and his second epistle; as is, I think, clear from several passages which I cannot conceive how the wit of man could detort to another meaning. Such is this in the fourth chapter—[d] *every spirit which confesseth that* Jesus Christ *is come in the flesh is of God; and every spirit which confesseth not that* Jesus Christ *is come in the flesh is not of God: and this is that spirit of* Anti-Christ *whereof ye have heard that it should come:* and this likewise in the second epistle—[e] *many deceivers are gone out into the world who confess not that*

[d] V. 2, 3.   [e] V. 7.

Jesus Christ is come in the flesh. *'This is a deceiver and* an Anti-Christ. It is, I conceive, with a view to this heresy that our Apostle in his gospel having observed that ^g *when the soldiers saw that Christ was dead they brake not his legs, but* that *one of the soldiers with a spear pierced his side and forthwith came thereout blood and water—* having, I say, observed this he adds—*he that saw it bare record, and his record is true, and he knoweth that he saith true that ye might believe.* But what were they to believe? what doctrine did this fact prove, that the Apostle takes so much care to testify and ascertain it? It could be an evidence of nothing else but that *Christ* had a *true and real* human body, and was *truly and really* dead, against the heretics of those times. To this testimony of *water and blood* our Apostle in his first epistle adds that of the *spirit*, the Holy Ghost, who at the baptism of *Christ* declar-

---

^f Ὡς μὴ ὁμολογοῦντων τὸν χριστὸν ἐν σαρκὶ ἐληλυθότα Ἀντιχρίστων ὑπαρχόντων. *As if he had said those that confess not that Jesus Christ is come in the flesh are Antichrists.* Epiph. speaking of this heresy. *hær.* xxvi. 15.

^g *John* xviii. 34, 35, 36.

SERMON V.

ed him to be the *son of God*; *for*, says he, *the spirit is truth*; and therefore could not give his attestation to an illusive scenical representation, [h] as these heretics affirmed his baptism in particular to have been.

I am persuaded that by carrying this in our minds we shall be able to understand, and feel the force and propriety of, many places in scripture which without such a reference appear either obscure or of no great importance; it will certainly furnish us with a very pertinent answer to that otherwise difficult question, so often and so strongly urged by the unitarians [i]; " why St. *John* (who on account of his

---

[h] Some of them held that *Jesus* and *Christ* were two different persons: that *Jesus* was born like other men from *Joseph* and *Mary*; but that at his baptism *Christ* descended into him in the shape of a dove, and deserted him again before his passion, leaving him to be crucified, &c. See *Irenæus* l. i. c. 25, &c. To this our Apostle alludes, c. ii. v. 22. *Who is a liar but he that denieth that* Jesus is the Christ? and c. v. v. 1, &c.

[i] It is observable, says Dr. *Whitby* in his preface to this gospel, that whereas *Crellius* in his book *de uno deo patre* Sect. ii. reckons up 36 arguments against the divinity of *Christ*, and *Woltzogenius* in his *præparatio ad utilem lectionem librorum* N. T. reckons up 60 against it, one half of them are taken from some passages of this gospel.

" sublime

"sublime description of the divine nature and eternity of the *word* obtained
the name of *the divine*) should notwithstanding afford more arguments
for his humanity than all the other
Evangelists?" When the other Evangelists wrote, the faith had not been op-
pugned; but St. *John*, who lived a long
while after them, had two different and
contradictory opinions to contend with.
Those therefore who deny the *divinity* of
our Saviour very artfully pass over the
arguments which he urges against their
predecessors, and eagerly press into their
service all the texts which, in opposition
to the other heresy, respect his *human nature* and that inferiority, which in the
oeconomy of our redemption he was
pleased to take upon him. His gospel
was written when *gnosticism* was at its
height, and therefore I presume intended
to confute that as well as the heresy of
Cerinthus and *Ebion*, who ran in the opposite extreme. Against these he first asserts
the *divinity* of our, Saviour saying that [k] *in*

[k] *John* i. 1.

SERMON V.

the beginning was the word, and the word was with God, and the word was God; and then maintains his *humanity* againſt the other heretics ſubjoining, [1] *the word was made fleſh and dwelt among us, and we beheld his glory;* appealing to the ſenſes, as he does in my text, for the certainty and reality of his incarnation.

This denial of Chriſt's real appearance in the fleſh, however ridiculous it appears to us, prevailed much and ſadly afflicted the church for the firſt two hundred years. It is taken notice of by [m] *Ignatius* biſhop of *Antioch* and cotemporary with our Apoſtle, who tells us that ſome abſented themſelves on that account from public prayers and the euchariſt: and it might, if it were neceſſary, be purſued through

---

[1] *John* i. 14. *Irenæus* after quoting thoſe paſſages out of our Apoſtle's *Epiſtles* which I have cited above, adds— Hæc autem ſimilia ſunt illi quod in *Evangelio* dictum eſt, quoniam *Verbum caro factum eſt et habitavit in nobis.* Iren. l. iii. c. 18.

[m] Τινὲς ἄθεοι ὄντες, τυτέϛιν ἄπιϛοι, λέγυσιν τὸ δοκεῖν πεπον-θέναι αὐτόν. *Ignat. ad Trall. et ad Smyrn.*

Εὐχαριϛίας κỳ προσευχῆς ἀπέχονται διὰ τὸ μὴ ὁμολογεῖν τὴν εὐχαριϛίαν σάρκα εἶναι τῶ σωτῆρος ἡμῶν Ἰησοῦ Χριϛοῦ τὴν ὑπὲρ ἁμαρτιῶν ἡμῶν παθοῦσαν. *Ignat. ad Smyrn.*

the writings of all the other fathers to even beyond the times of *Irenæus* and *Tertullian;* the latter of whom wrote a treatise professedly against it, entitled " *De* " *Carne Christi:*" in which he makes use of this remarkable argument.—[a] *Those,* says he, *who think that Christ's incarnation was only in appearance destroy the resurrection of the flesh. If his human nature is not allowed, how can his death be asserted? If his death is not allowed, neither can his resurrection be maintained. But if the resurrection of Christ is overthrown, ours falls of course.* This argument, I say, is remarkable; because it shews how intimately connected this article of *Christ's humanity* is with the hope of a Christian; and because it is evidently the same which St. *Paul* makes use of in his *fifteenth* chapter of the *first* epistle to the *Corinthians;* and is therefore a strong presumption that the Apostle there defends the resurrection of

---

[a] Qui carnem Christi putativam putant resurrectionem carnis infringunt. Si Caro ejus negatur, quomodo mors ejus asseveratur? Negatâ vero morte, nec de resurrectione constabit. Proinde resurrectione Christi it firmatâ etiam nostra subversa est. To the same purpose St. *Cyril,* εἰ φάντασμα ἦν ἡ ἐνανθρώπησις φάντασμα κὴ ἡ σωτηρία. *Cat.* iv. 6.

the

the body against the same heretics; and for the same reason he joins in another place *Christ's incarnation and resurrection*, as truths depending upon each other; charging *Timothy* to preach and inculcate them—°*remember that Jesus Christ of the seed of David was raised from the dead.*

Whilst the miracles of our Saviour, and more particularly his resurrection, were fresh in the memory of men; there could be, there was no doubt in the church about his *divinity*: of this period therefore the enemy of mankind took advantage by tempting them to deny his *humanity* and the infirmities and sufferings consequent, as inconsistent with the excellence of his person: but, when the sense of them began to wear out of men's minds, he boldly ventured one step further and tempted them to deny his *divinity*. By the *first* heresy his sacrifice was entirely exploded; by the *second* rendered of no effect. The first has long ago been entirely forgotten; but the second having come down even to our times under different modifications, it

° 2 *Tim.* ii. 8.

cannot be an useless or disagreeable employment to enquire into the proofs contained in the evangelical and apostolical writings of that *divinity,* which our church maintains against all *unitarians* whatsoever.

In order to do this in as clear and distinct a manner as I can, I shall proceed gradually; and consider

> First, our Saviour's *pre-existence in general.*
>
> Secondly, his *temporal,*
>
> And thirdly, his *eternal pre-existence.*

As the *first* particular is included in both the others, I need not labour for arguments to prove it. I shall therefore content myself with quoting a few plain passages, which have a *general* reference to this doctrine. Thus from *Christ's* saying to his disciples, *ᵖ as my father has sent me so send I you,* we may fairly infer that he, as well as the Apostles, had a being before he had his mission. When he tells the

ᵖ *John* xx. 21.

Jews,

Jews, [q] *I know whence I came,* he evidently speaks of some place and state of life prior to that into which he came: What this place was he tells them soon after.—[r] *I proceeded forth and came from God.* When he said that [s] *he came down from heaven,* not only the *Jews* understood him as speaking of a *real descent, Is not this Jesus the son of Joseph whose father and mother we know? How is it then that he saith, I came down from heaven?* but he himself ascertains that meaning by urging to them, *What and if you shall see the son of man ascend up where he was before?* In which passage he plainly asserts that " his ascen-
" sion into heaven would be but a tranf-
" lation of the human nature thither
" where according to a more excellent
" nature he did abide before his incar-
" nation."

From the frequent application of the term *coming* to our blessed Saviour it has been imagined, and not without reason, that he is emphatically stiled the ὁ ἐρχόμενος *he that is coming, he that cometh.* When

[q] John viii. 14.   [r] John viii. 42.
[s] John vi. 38. 42. 62.

John's

John's disciples enquired of him if he was the *Messiah*; ^t *they said unto him art thou the* ὁ ἐρχόμενος. ^u *The multitude cried, Hosannah to the son of David; Blessed be the* ὁ ἐρχόμενος. ^w *Verily I say unto you, you shall not see me, until the time when you shall say, Blessed be the* ὁ ἐρχόμενος. The *Messiah* had been so stiled before by the prophet ^x *Habakkuc* in a passage alluded to by St. *Paul*, *Yet a little while and* the ὁ ἐρχόμενος *he that is coming will come.*

I shall quote but one passage out of the epistles relating to Christ's pre-existence in general; but that one is so full and clear that though it stood alone it would be sufficient to establish the doctrine. St. *Paul* recommends our Saviour to the *Philippians* as a pattern of humility, ^y *who being in the form of God — took upon him the form of a servant.* Whatever is the precise meaning of this passage, thus much is undeniable; that there is a contrast, in which lies the whole force of the example

---

^t *Matth.* xi. 3. ^u *Matth.* xxi. 9.
^w *Luke* xiii. 35. ^x *Habak.* ii. 3. *Heb.* 10. 37.
^y *Philip.* ii. 6, 7.

proposed,

propofed, between that ſtate in which *Chriſt* was *before* and that in which he was *after* he had taken upon him our nature; and confequently that he had a being before he was born of the virgin *Mary*. Accordingly we read in the new teſtament of feveral *particular* periods of time in which he did pre-exiſt.

The *firſt* period of Chriſt's *temporal pre-exiſtence* mentioned in the new teſtament is the time of *David*, about a thoufand years before he was born. *Jeſus* afked the Phariſees, [z] *what think ye of Chriſt? whoſe ſon is he? they ſay unto him, the ſon of David; he ſaith unto them, how then doth David in ſpirit call him Lord; ſaying the Lord ſaid unto my Lord, ſit thou on my right hand till I make thine enemies thy footſtool? If David call him Lord how is he his ſon? And no man was able to anſwer him a word.* It is plain from hence that the perfon whom *David* calls *Lord* was then in being; and that he was the *Meſſiah*,

[z] *Matth.* xxii. 42, &c.

contrary

contrary to the artifice of later Jews [a] who apply this pfalm to *Ezechias*, is afferted by our Saviour and allowed by the Pharifees themfelves.

The *next* period in which we read of the pre-exiftence of *Chrift* carries us about four hundred years higher. For St. *Paul*, laying before the *Corinthians* the fpecial favours and advantages vouchfafed to the Jews during their abode in the wildernefs, warns them not to truft too much upon the like fpiritual privileges, nor to commit thofe fins which were the caufe of their ruin, and particularly [b] *not to tempt* Chrift *as fome of them alfo tempted him.*

[c] It was the univerfal belief not only of the primitive Chriftians, but likewife the ancient Jews, that it was the *Meffiah* who conducted the *Ifraelites* by the pillar of cloud and of fire. [d] *Behold,* fays God, *I*

---

[a] See *Juftin Martyr's* dialogue againft *Trypho*, p. 251. Ed. *Jebb.* and likewife *Tertullian adv. Mar.* l. v. c. 9.
[b] 1 *Cor.* x. 9.
[c] See Dr. *Allix in his judgment of the Jewifh church,* c. 13, 14, 15. and Mr. *Lowth* on *Ifaiah* lxiii. 9.
[d] *Exod.* xxiii. 20, 21.

fend

SERMON V.

send an angel before thee to keep thee in the way, and to bring thee into the place which I have prepared; beware of him and obey his voice, provoke him not; for he will not pardon your transgressions, for my name is in him. He is here indeed called *an Angel*; but it is at the same time declared that he had power to pardon transgressions, and that in him was the name of God. And accordingly the incommunicable name *Jehovah* is given to him.—*ᵉ Jehovah went before the people in a pillar of cloud by day and of fire by night*; and *ᶠ Jehovah looked unto the host of the Egyptians through the pillar of fire and the cloud.* It could not therefore be a created Angel, for which of them has power to pardon sins? in which of them is the name of God? It was ᵍ *the Angel of the covenant, the* ʰ *Angel of God's presence*; an Angel by office not nature: *the Captain of the Lord's host*; which title when *Joshua* heard ⁱ *he fell on his face and did worship and said unto him, what saith my Lord unto his servant?* It was he who

---

ᵉ *Exod.* xiii. 21. ᶠ *Exod.* xiv. 24.
ᵍ *Mal.* iii. 1.   ʰ *Is.* lxiii. 9.
ⁱ *Josh.* v. 14.

took

took up his refidence over the ark, whofe *k glory filled the tabernacle* which *Mofes* built according to his promife and prediction in that divinely-infpired fong of praife and thankfgiving to God for his wonderful deliverance of his people.—*l The Lord is my ftrength and my falvation; he is my God and I fhall prepare him an habitation.* Of this glorious refidence the bleffing conferred by *Noah* upon *Shem* was undoubtedly prophetical.—*m God fhall dwell in the tabernacles of Shem;* and its further application to our bleffed Saviour is confirmed by St. *John* when, in manifeft allufion to this habitation and the glory by which the Lord manifefted his prefence, he fays *n the Word was made flefh and* ἐσκήνωσε dwelt in a tabernacle *among us, and we beheld his* glory, *the glory of the only begotten fon of the father.*

The *next period* in which the fcriptures of the new teftament take notice of the pre-exiftence of *Chrift* is indefinite; but

k *Exod.* xl. 35.
m *Genef.* ix. 27.
l *Exod.* xv. 2.
n *John* i. 14.

the

the antiquity of it is so far ascertained that it is expressly asserted to have been before Abraham. ° *Your father Abraham,* says *Christ* to the Jews, *rejoiced to see my day, and he saw it and was glad: then said the Jews, thou art not yet fifty years old and hast thou seen Abraham? Jesus said unto them, verily, verily, I say unto you,* before *Abraham* was I am. It is amazing what pains the enemies of this doctrine have taken to elude and perplex this most clear and plain passage. Some interpret it thus —*Before Abraham is made,* what his name signifies, *a father of many nations* I am the Messiah. Others take the words πρὶν Ἀβραὰμ γενέσθαι in their natural meaning; but to the others they add a strange qualification, *before Abraham was born, I was in God's foreknowledge and decree.* Every one of *Christ's* hearers was before *Abraham* in the same sense. Why then should they be so exasperated as to *take up stones to cast at him?* Doubtless because they understood his words in their literal and obvious sense, as a direct answer to

° *John* viii. 56, 57, 58.

their

their question which respected only actual existence. In this respect our Saviour asserting a priority appeared to them to assert in fact an eternal existence; and for that reason they attempted to inflict upon him [p] the punishment which the law decreed against blasphemy. I know that the expressions *(Abraham rejoiced to see my day and he saw it)* are generally understood in a metaphorical and religious sense, *he saw it with the eye of faith as a thing to be accomplished in future ages.* I verily believe that *Abraham* did see the day of *Christ* with the eye of faith; but I do not take that to be our Saviour's meaning in this place; for then *Abraham* must have seen him only as one who was to come; and therefore his priority of existence to *Abraham*, which is here asserted, would be not only foreign but in a great degree contradictory to the occasion on which it is introduced. I cannot therefore but con-

---

[p] *He that blasphemeth the name of the Lord, he shall surely be put to death, and all the congregation shall certainly stone him.* Levit. xxiv. 16. Thus in the 10th chap. when he says, *I and the Father are one, the Jews took up stones again to stone him.* v. 30, 31.

clude that *Christ* here alludes to his frequent, and more especially to two illustrious, manifestations of himself to the father of the faithful. The first was in the plains of *Mamre*, when he came attended by two Angels in the form and likeness of man: And ^q *Jehovah appeared unto him—and he lift up his eyes and looked, and lo! three men stood by him.* Of two of them the patriarch takes no notice; but to the third he addresses himself, calls him ^r *Lord, the judge of all the earth*, and pleads with him for the cities of *Pentapolis*. ^s *Behold now I have taken upon me to speak unto the Lord, who am but dust and ashes. Oh let not the Lord be angry and I will speak.* This person, whose divine majesty is acknowledged by *Abraham* and allowed by himself, who has the sacred name *Jehovah* given him by ^t *Moses*, he surely could not be a mere man or created angel; neither could he be God the Father; for ^u *him no man hath seen at any time.* We may therefore, with all primitive antiquity, conclude

^q *Genes.* xviii. 1, 2. See *Just. Mart. Dial.* p. 367.
^r V. 25.   ^s V. 27. 30.
^t V. 22.   ^u John i. 18.

that it was that God who afterwards appeared unto *[w] Isaac,* and called himself *the God of his father Abraham;* to *Jacob,* [x] and called himself *the God of Abraham and Isaac;* to [y] *Moses,* and called himself *the God of Abraham, Isaac, and Jacob;* who is by [z] St. Stephen called *the God of glory;* " he who always descended to converse with men from the beginning, setting before us the order of that dispensation which was afterwards manifested."— *He* thus appeared in a *human shape* to *Abraham,* as a prelude and symbol of his taking upon him *human nature,* to lay a foundation (says [a] *Tertullian*) for our faith, that we might the more readily believe that the Son of God was come into the world, when we knew he had formerly done so. The other appearance, in this place more particularly alluded to, was still more illustrious; for in it *Abraham,* having obeyed the command of God bidding him [b] *offer up his only begotten Son, of whom it had been said, that in Isaac shall thy seed be called,* received him

---

[w] *Genes.* xxvi. 24.
[y] *Exod.* iii. 15.
[a] *Tertull.* cont. *Prax.* c. 14.
[x] *Genes.* xxviii. 13.
[z] *Acts* vii. 2.
[b] *Heb.* ix. 17, 18, 19.

even

even from the dead in a figure: 'God being pleafed to reveal unto him by way of myftery, how that feed of his fhould make all the nations of the earth bleffed ; and therefore, for a perpetual memorial of this wonderful revelation, the grateful patriarch ^d called the place Jehovah-jireh, *becaufe in it Jehovah had been feen.*

The next period, in which the New Teftament mentions *Chrift's temporal pre-exiftence,* reaches beyond the flood. ^e *Chrift* (fays St. *Peter*) *hath once fuffered for fins— being put to death in the flefh, but quickened by the fpirit: by which alfo he went and preached* τοῖς ἐν Φυλακῇ πνεύμασι *to the fpirits* which are *now in prifon* (*referved,* as he fays in ^f another place, *unto judgment*) to

---

^c *Mede's Difc.* 13. 25.

^d *Genef.* xxii. 14. See Mr. *Shuckford's Connect.* v. II. p. 21.   ^e 1 *Pet.* iii. 18, 19, 20.

^f 2 *Pet.* ii. 4. By the confent of the Jewifh nation (fays Dr. *Whitby*) *The generation of the old world have no portion in the world to come, neither fhall they ftand up in judgment;* for it is faid, *My fpirit fhall not always ftrive with man*—i. e. according to Bifhop *Patrick,* My fpirit in my prophets *Enoch* and *Noah* fhall not always be endeavouring to bring men to repentance, but fhall proceed to punifh them. Now this punifhment, adds Dr. *W.* being the drowning of

them *Christ preached, when once the long-suffering of God waited in the days of Noah while the ark was preparing.* According to the natural and obvious explication of this passage, in which all the writers of primitive christianity agree, it was *Christ* who preached repentance to the old world by the ministry of his prophets: of whom *Noah* was one, being called by our apostle [g] *a preacher of righteousness;* and *Enoch* another, for St. [h] *Jude,* speaking of the ungodly in his days, says that to them was applicable the *prophecy* of *Enoch,* pronouncing a fearful destruction on the antediluvian sinners; *behold the Lord cometh with ten thousand of his saints to execute judgement,* &c.

Having thus clearly traced our Saviour's pre-existence as far back as the days of *Enoch,* it will not be difficult to conceive that he was the person who in the few generations preceding condescended to

the old world, *their spirits have been ever since kept in prison, or reserved in chains of darkness, to the judgement of the great day.*
[g] 2 *Pet.* ii. 5.   [h] *Jude* 14.

manifest

manifest himself to man. And herein we have not only the consentient testimonies of the catholic doctors, but of the *Arians* themselves. With him therefore did those walk who are said to have ⁱ *walked with God*; from ᵏ *his presence Cain*, after the murder of *Abel, went out; from his face he was hid*, because from that time he was excluded from his special protection: he never after this enjoyed that intercourse with the Mediator God, which he had been pleased to continue from the beginning. It was he who appeared to *Adam* immediately after the fall, whose voice when our first parents heard, ˡ *they hid themselves from the presence of the Lord God*. And according to this primitive divinity, the *Jerusalem Targum* reads *The* Word *of the Lord called Adam*; the *Targum* of *Onkelos* and *Jonathan*—*They heard the voice of the* Word *of the Lord God*. And indeed ᵐ " learned men have long since observed, that the " *Chaldee* paraphrases, almost " as often as mention is made in scripture

---

ⁱ *Genes.* v. 24.   ᵏ *Genes.* iv. 14. 16.
ˡ *Genes.* iii. 8, 9.
ᵐ See Bishop *Bull's Defence of the Nicene Faith*, p. 28.

" of

"of God speaking with us, assisting us, and conversing with us, have rendered the name of God by (*the Word*)", signifying, that in those places the scripture treated of *the Son of God*, who is called *the Word*. He it was to whom God the Father said, [n] *Behold the man is become as one of us;* with whom he, as it were, consulted when he said, [o] *let us make man:* upon which passage *Epiphanius* observes—*This is the language of* God *to his* Word *and only begotten, as all the faithful believe.*

This *Word* or only begotten Son of God was not only pre-existent, as we have already seen from scripture, within a few days of the beginning; but, if we believe the same scripture, in the very beginning,

---

[n] *Genes.* iii. 22.
[o] *Genes.* i. 26. See Bishop *Patrick.* Idem ipse qui ab initio psalmavit *Adam*, cum quo et loquebatur pater, *faciamus hominem secundum imaginem et similitudinem nostram,* in novissimis temporibus se ipsum manifestans hominibus, &c. *Iren. advers. hær.* l. 5. c. 15. *Tertullian* calls it *Præfatio patris ad filium.* de *resurr. carn.* c. 26. Almost all the fathers indeed bring this passage in proof of *Christ*'s pre-existence; θέλεις γνῶναι ὅτι σὺν τῷ πατρὶ καὶ πρὸ τῆς ἐνανθρωπήσεως ἐςι Χριςὸς κύριος-ἠλθὲ ἐπὶ τὴν πρώτην ἔςοδον τὴν γένεσιν. Ποιήσωμεν ἄνθρωπον, ὂ κατ' εἰκόνα ΕΜΗΝ, ἀλλὰ κατ' εἰκόνα ΗΜΕΤΕΡΑΝ. *Cyrill. Catech.* x. c. 4.

before

before the creation, before time itself: for time and the world began together, time being the measure of the existence of one sensible thing by the duration of another sensible thing. That he was *in the beginning* is expressly asserted by St. *John*; and that that phrase is in the Hebrew language equivalent to being *from eternity*, is acknowledged by *Grotius*. This the Evangelist repeats twice, and then adds as a proof of it, that *all things were made by him, and* that *without him was not any thing made that was made.* Human reason itself will teach us, that the creator must be prior to the thing created, the cause to the effect. We see how careful St. *John* is, lest we should in any way confine or restrain this creation; for he first *positively* asserts, that all things were made by him, and then *negatively,* that *without* him was not any thing made that was made. And for the same reason St. *Paul* comprehensively tells us, that *by him all things were created that are in heaven and that are in earth, visible and invisible, whether they be*

ᵖ *John* i. 1.   ᑫ *Coloss.* i. 16.

thrones

thrones, or dominions, or principalities, or powers; all things were created by him and for him; and he is before all things, and by him all things consist.

From this eternal pre-existence and this act of creation our Saviour's *divine nature* is apparent. He that made all things out of nothing could not be less than God. And for this very reason our apostle gives *Christ* the pre-eminence above *Moses*, ' *inasmuch as he who builded the house hath more honour than the house; for every house is builded by some man, but he that built all things is God.* In the passage cited before he is carefully distinguished, not only from the visible and material, but moreover from the spiritual and invisible creation, from *thrones, and dominions, and principalities, and powers;* by which titles all angels, and archangels, and the whole host of heaven are comprised. He could not therefore be one of them, as the *Arians* fondly dream; but that *Word* who ' *in the beginning was with God and was God.* The name

---

' *Heb.* iii. 3, 4.   ' *John* i. 1, 2.

Jehovah,

SERMON V.

Jehovah, the proper and incommunicable name of God, was given to him in all his appearances to the Patriarchs, as [t] the ancient fathers prove at large in their writings against the Jews. By the same title he is described by the prophets [u] *Isaiah*, [w] *Hosea*, [x] *Zachariah*, [y] *Malachi*; and particularly by [z] *Jeremiah*, when prophecying of him under the name of *the branch of David*, he says, *In his days Judah shall be saved, and Israel shall dwell safely; and this is his name, whereby he shall be called*, Jehovah *our righteousness*. He is called [a] *the Lord over all*, [b] *God*, [c] *the true God*, [d] *the great God*. In him [e] *the fullness of the God-*

---

[t] The fathers of the first ages in general teach, that the Son of God frequently appeared to the holy men under the Old Testament; yea they explain all those appearances in which the name *Jehovah* and divine honours are given to him that appears (although at other times he is called the Angel, or an Angel) of this very Son of God. He is a stranger in the fathers who knows not this.—B. *Bull's Def.* p. 14. This assertion he proves by quotations from *Just. Iren. Clem.* &c. &c.

[u] *Is.* xl. 10.—xlviii. 17.
[x] *Zech.* ii. 10, 11.
[z] *Jerem.* xxiii. 6.
[b] *Rom.* xiv. 12. *Heb.* i. 8.—iii. 4.
[c] 1 *John* v. 20.
[e] *Col.* ii. 9.

[w] *Hos.* i. 7.
[y] *Mal.* iii. 1.
[a] *Rom.* x. 12.
[d] *Tit.* ii. 13.

head

head is said to dwell: 'God protests by his prophet *Isaiah*, that he *will not give his glory to another*; but *Christ* did really participate of his glory even before the beginning of the world; for he saith in his human nature—*Now father glorify me with the glory which I had with thee before the world was.* The same prophet was honoured with a vision of [g] *the Lord sitting upon his throne—and above it stood the seraphim—and one cried unto another and said, holy, holy, holy, is the Lord of hosts; the whole earth is full of his glory.* Now we are expressly told by St. [h] *John,* that in this illustrious vision it was the *glory of Christ* that the prophet saw. *Christ* therefore is the *Lord of hosts,* the *Jehovah Zebaoth*; whose glory the *seraphim* sung, as they did afterwards in the revelation vouchsafed to [i] St. *John,* saying, *holy, holy, holy, Lord God Almighty, which was, and is, and is to come.* These titles he himself challenges —[k] *I am Alpha and Omega, the beginning and the ending,*

---

[f] Compare *Is.* xlii. 8. and xlviii. 11. with *John* xvii. 5.
[g] *Is.* vi. 1, 2, 3.   [h] *John* xii. 41.
[i] *Revel.* iv. 8.   [k] *Revel.* i. 8.

saith

faith the Lord, which is, and which was, and which is to come; the Almighty.

No nature except the divine is capable of divine attributes; yet they are all ascribed to *Christ*. That he is *the creator of all things,* and therefore *before* all things, we have already seen. That he is *omniscient* St. *Peter* teaches us when he says, [1] *Lord thou knowest all things*; and St. *Paul* assures us, [m] that *in him are hidden all the treasures of wisdom and knowledge,* and that [n] *he both will bring to light the hidden things of darkness, and will make manifest the counsels of the heart.* "God alone knows the hearts of " all men; yet *Christ* expressly claims " this knowledge to himself, by saying " [o] *all the churches shall know that I am* " *he which searcheth the reins and the hearts,* " *and I will give to every one of you ac-* " *cording to your works.*" He is *omnipresent*; for he promises that, [p] *wherever two or three are gathered together in his name, he will be present in the midst of them.* Lastly,

[l] *John* xxi. 17.
[n] 1 *Cor.* iv. 5.
[p] *Matt.* xviii. 20.
[m] *Coloss.* ii. 3.
[o] *Revel.* ii. 29.

he

he is *omnipotent*; for [q] *he is* not only *the wisdom* but also *the power of God*; [r] *he is able even to subdue all things to himself*, and [s] *whatever things the father doth, these also doth the son likewise; for as the father raiseth up the dead and quickeneth them, even so the Son quickeneth whom he will; for the Father judgeth no man, but hath committed all judgement to the Son.* From hence I argue in the words immediately following, words spoken by our blessed Saviour himself, that [t] *all men should honour the Son even as they honour the Father.* God is a jealous god, and will not suffer the honour peculiar to himself to be transferred to another. — It is written, [u] *Thou shalt worship the Lord thy God, and him only shalt thou serve:* yet [w] *when he bringeth his first-begotten into the world, he saith, let all the angels of God worship him.* The *Socinians* themselves acknowledge religious worship to be due to *Christ:* but to what purpose do they worship him? for if he is not God, he is

[q] 1 *Cor.* i. 24.   [r] *Phil.* iii. 21.
[s] *John* v. 19, 20, 21. εἰ δὲ ἡ δύναμις αὐτὴ ἰσόδηλον ὅτι καὶ οὐσία. *Chrysost. in Joan.* 10. 30.
[t] *John* v. 23.   [u] *Matt.* iv. 10.
[w] *Heb.* i. 6.

not

not omnipresent to hear, nor omnipotent to save them. They indeed make him a God, a nuncupative or titular God, a God by grace and office, not by nature; and by this distinction endeavour to clear themselves from idolatry; but in vain: it is the very crime with which the apostle charges the heathen, [x] *they did service to them which are not gods by nature.* We read no where in scripture of religious adoration paid to a creature. [y] St. *John* indeed twice owns that *he fell at the feet of an angel to worship him:* but he was rebuked; and it is probable that he took him for *the angel of the covenant,* the *Word of God,* which had so often before his incarnation appeared in the shape of an angel, and might therefore be thought by the apostle to appear so after his ascension: and the words of the angel, when attentively considered, seem to convey this idea —*See thou do it not; I am thy fellow-servant*— i. e. I am not that Angel which thou takest me to be—*worship God.*

[x] *Gal.* iv. 8.   [y] *Revel.* xix. 10.—xxii. 9.

This mystery of the union of two such infinitely distant natures as the divine and human in our blessed Saviour, so clearly revealed in the word of God, is so sublime and abstruse, that I hesitate not a moment to confess my utter inability to explain or comprehend it. When we consider things belonging unto God, we ought never to forget making a distinction between giving a reason for our *belief* and a reason of the *thing believed*. To the first our understanding is always commensurate; the other may be and often is of such a nature, as renders it absolutely impossible to be the object of human knowledge. Who can comprehend, and yet who doubts of, the self-existence, eternity, infinity, and omnipresence of God? Who can explain the manner in which cold clay is fitted to receive and preserve a vital union with the soul? Yet that there is such an union every one of us feels, and nobody in his senses ever attempted to deny. If therefore, in things pertaining to man, man requires not perfect knowledge, why in things supernatural and divine should his [z] *lofty*

[z] *2 Cor.* x. 5.

imagination exalt itself against the knowledge of God? Why should he not think it as possible that *God and man should make one Christ,* as that *the reasonable soul and body make one man?*

That this great mystery however, tho' far above reason, is not contradictory to it is evident from the opinion, which obtained universally among the heathen, of their gods appearing in human shape; an opinion which occasioned *the men of Lystra,* when they saw the miracles done by *Paul* and *Barnabas,* to cry out, [a] *The gods are come down to us in the likeness of men.*

There seems in general to be a congruity in the reason of things, that a mediator *by office* should likewise be a mediator *by nature;* one nearly allied to and having a common interest with both the parties, who by his interposal are to be reconciled; credit with the superior who is offended, and sympathy for the offender.

[a] *Acts* xiv. 11.

There appears to be a particular propriety in the designation of the *Word* to the work of our redemption, that he should give man a new life who first gave him his being; that the image of God upon our souls should be repaired by him who is the express image of God; that through the alone interposition of the *true and essential* Son, we should receive an *adoptive* sonship, be make partakers of the inheritance; [b] *heirs of God and joint-heirs with Christ.*

It seems expedient that our Redeemer should have been made *man,* that the same nature which had sinned should likewise suffer; and [c] " that as mankind by *man overcome* was made obnoxious to death, so by *man overcoming* we should rise to life." This is evidently the apostle's argument, when he says to the *Hebrews*— [d] *it became him*—*bringing many sons to glory, to make the captain of their salvation perfect through sufferings; for both he that sanctifieth and*

---

[b] Rom. viii. 17. *God sent his son*—*that we might receive the adoption of sons.* Gal. iv. 4, 5.
[c] Iren. L. v. c. 22.   [d] Heb. ii. 10, 11.

they

SERMON V.

they who are sanctified are all of one, i. e. nature or condition ; *for which cause he is not ashamed to call them brethren :* and again, ** forasmuch as the children are partakers of flesh and blood, he also himself took part of the same, that* through death *he might destroy him who had the power of death*, &c. Thus did *Christ*'s human nature qualify him for suffering ; but his sufferings must acquire their worth and value from some higher quality : and surely nothing but the dignity which belonged to it, by virtue of its union with the godhead, could make his blood so precious, his sacrifice so meritorious, as to expiate and satisfy his father's justice for the sins of the whole world.

Christ is the mediator not only of *redemption*, but likewise of *intercession*; and we may discover a fitness why in that character he should partake of both natures. His being *man* makes him more inclined, thro' an experimental sense of our infirmities, to pity and succour us ; and we, knowing that we have an intercessor of our own na-

^e *Heb.* ii. 14.

ture at the right hand of God, may approach him with assurance of mercy. It was moreover requisite that he should be *God*; that the dignity of his person, and his relation with the Father, might add weight to his intercession and confidence to our faith. ᶠ *We have not an high priest who cannot be touched with the feeling of our infirmities, but one who was in all points tempted as we are, yet without sin.* ᵍ *He continuing for ever hath an unchangeable priesthood; wherefore he is able to save them to the uttermost that come unto God by him, seeing he ever liveth to make intercession for us.* I am well aware of the advantage which Papists are wont to take of the distinction here made; by asserting, that though there be but *one* mediator of *redemption*, yet there may be *many* mediators of *intercession*. But upon what text of scripture do they found this assertion? We are there taught in express words that ʰ *that there is one God, and one mediator between God and men, the man Christ Jesus: one God,* in opposition to the many

---

ᶠ *Heb.* iv. 15.   ᵍ *Heb.* vii. 24, 25.
ʰ 1 *Tim.* ii. 5.

heathen

heathen deities; *one mediator*, in opposition to that multitude of inferior *demons*, whom [i] philosophers looked upon as mediators between gods and men. But to us, as there is but one God, so is there also but one mediator; who, as our *sacrifice, redeemed* us by shedding his blood upon the cross; and, as our *high-priest*, in virtue of his blood thus shed, *intercedes* for us for ever in heaven. [k] *For though there be that are called Gods, whether in heaven or in earth (as there be Gods many and Lords many) but to us there is but one God the Father, of whom are all things, and we in him; and one Lord Jesus Christ, by whom are all things, and we by him.*

It was he who from the beginning took under his special protection, comforted, and blessed the faithful of all ages. Surely he, whose [l] *delights were in the sons of men* while they were enemies, will not now,

---

[i] Θεὸς ἀνθρώπῳ ὀ μίγνυται, ἀλλὰ διὰ ΔΑΙΜΟΝΩΝ πᾶσά ἐστιν ἡ ὁμιλία κ̓ ἡ διάλεκτ͠ος θεοῖς πρὸς ἀνθρώπους. *Plat. in Sympos.*
Τὸ ΔΑΙΜΟΝΩΝ γίνος ἐν μέσῳ θεῶν κ̓ ἀνθρώπων. *Plut. de def. Orac.*

[k] 1 Cor. viii. 5, 6.   [l] Prov. viii. 31.

when he has reconciled them to God, cease to love and cherish them? He who guided and protected the church which ᵐ *was not called by his name*, how much more will he now, when he is solemnly proclaimed and acknowledged its head, preside over it, be its guardian, director, and defender? ⁿ *Who is he that condemneth? it is Christ that died, yea rather that is risen again, who is even at the right hand of God, who also maketh intercession for us.* ᵒ *Let us therefore come boldly unto the throne of grace, that we may obtain mercy, and find grace in the time of need:* for ᵖ *To him that overcometh will he grant to sit with him in his throne, even as he also overcame and is sit down with his Father in his throne.*

ᵐ *If.* lxiii. 19.   ⁿ *Rom.* viii. 34.
ᵒ *Heb.* iv. 16.   ᵖ *Revel.*iii. 21.

SERMON VI.

1 Cor. xi. 19.

There must be also heresies among you.

WAS it not for the goodness of God, which turns those things which are poisons of nature into medicines of grace; a zealous Christian could not but be overwhelmed with melancholy reflections, upon observing with how much difficulty the mind of man is worked upon to embrace, and how easily persuaded to forsake, spiritual and divine truths. In all the works of *art*, time is required before the seeds of decay are introduced; but in those of *grace*, scarcely is the building raised, but the beauty of it is defaced by some

some disorder, the pillars shaken by schism, the foundation undermined by heresy, and the whole fabric in danger of being overthrown by apostacy and infidelity. I pass over the fatal seduction of our first parents, and the numerous instances in which their genuine offspring but too faithfully copied after their pattern during the Mosaical dispensation. History, both sacred and profane, is full of the earnest expectation with which the Jews looked for redemption in *Israel* by the promised *Messiah:* yet, when this object of all their wishes and hopes appeared amongst them, with what obstinacy and prejudice did they reject him and his doctrine? They were indeed the first *converts*; but they were likewise the first *apostates*. Scarce was the good *seed* sown, but [a] *thorns sprang up with it, and choaked it.* Many fell off totally and finally from the gospel: the few that remained were unsettled and wavering; false prophets arose among them, [b] *handling the word of God deceitfully*, and [c] *corrupting* the

[a] *Luke* viii. 7.   [b] 2 *Cor.* iv. 2.
[c] 2 *Cor.* xi. 3.

SERMON VI.

minds of others *from the simplicity that is in Christ.* Diversities of opinions were introduced; feuds, animosities, and schisms followed; unity was turned into division, the peace of the gospel into spiritual war.

[d] *If these things were done in a green tree, what must it be in the dry?* If the husbandry of God planted and watered by the apostles did, even whilst they were alive, thus abound with tares; how could it be expected that, under the care of their successors, it should be exempted from them? Indeed the reverse is but too well attested. Even *Jerusalem,* [e] the mother of us all, this primogenial church (which for fifteen successions was governed by our Lord's kindred) [f] remained no longer a virgin, than while she was under the tuition of *James* his brother: she was, immediately

---

[d] *Luke* xxiii. 31.

[e] Μήτηρ ἁπασῶν τῶν ἐκκλησιῶν ἡ ἐν Ἱεροσολύμοις. *Conc. Const. in Syn. Ep.*

[f] Μετὰ τὸ μαρτυρῆσαι Ἰάκωβον τὸν δίκαιον ὡς καὶ ὁ κύριος ἐπὶ τῷ αὐτῷ λόγῳ, πάλιν ὁ ἐκ θείου αὐτοῦ Σιμεὼν ὁ τοῦ Κλωπᾶ καθίσταται ἐπίσκοπος· ὃν προέθεντο πάντες ὄντα ἀνεψιὸν τοῦ κυρίου δεύτερον· διὰ τοῦτο ἐκάλουν τὴν ἐκκλησίαν παρθένον· οὔπω γὰρ ἐφθαρτο ἀκοαῖς ματαίαις· ἄρχεται δ' ὁ Θεόδοτις, διὰ τὸ μὴ γενέσθαι αὐτὸν ἐπίσκοπον, ὑποφθείρειν. *Euseb. Ecc. Hist.* L. iv. c. 22.

upon his death, corrupted with strange adulterous doctrines by *Thebuthis*, whose pride could not brook having *Simeon* the son of *Cleopas* preferred to the bishoprick before him. That every other church was infested with them, cannot be denied by any one who is at all conversant with the writings of the primitive fathers, whose pious labours were chiefly directed against the [g] heresies prevailing in their times; which, though resisted by the constancy and zeal of many learned champions of Christianity, spread their baleful poison far and near; insomuch that, as [h] *Eusebius* tells us in his life of *Constantine*, the disputes and divisions among Christians rose to that height, that the pagans took occasion from them to expose publickly upon the stage the venerable doctrines of divine truth to the most indecent laughter and ridicule.

Of these and subsequent divisions modern infidels likewise have not failed to take advantage; urging, that the diversity

[g] *Epiphanius*, in a book written for that purpose, gives an account of *eighty* heresies which grew up with the gospel.
[h] L. ii. c. 61.

of opinions among Christians affects the truth of Christianity itself, is a proof of the uncertainty at least of the divine authority it pretends to, and renders its principles precarious and problematical.

To this argument against the gospel of *Christ* the church of *Rome* gives great countenance, by strenuously contending that *Unity* among the members is a necessary mark of the *true* Church; which title she on that account arrogates to herself, and denies to the reformed churches; to ours in particular, because of the different opinions maintained within it, and the various sects and irreconcileable communions that have gone out from it.

To the infidel we may observe, that the disputes and controversies among Christians are not about the grounds and principles of their religion, and therefore do not affect Christianity in general, the foundations of which remain unshaken: and though different human explications of some particular doctrines render the different acceptation of those doctrines dubious; yet it by
no

no means follows that the doctrines themselves, much less the truth of Christianity, which is acknowledged by all the disputants, is thereby rendered uncertain. There are, and always were, and (whilst our faculties remain limited) must necessarily ever be, various opinions in every other science as well as divinity: yet will any man from thence argue, that there are no certain principles any where; that speculations in philosophy are idle, and arts useless; that no man ought to attempt the recovery of his health or property; but that all human affairs, all concerns in civil and religious life, should stand still? We are told that there were in ancient *Rome* people from [i] six hundred different nations, who all followed a different way of worship: and in early *Greece* " there were as " many religions almost as men; for every " man's religion was his fancy." When

---

[i] For this fact Mr. *Collins*, in his *preface* to his *Discourse on the grounds*, &c. quotes *Lipsius*; but *Lipsius* only says almost six hundred, *sexcentæ nationes* pene *in urbem fluxerant. De magnit. Rom.* l. 4. c. 5. and this *Lipsius* in his turn asserts on the authority of *Dionysius* of *Halicarnassus*; whereas the historian only says *a very great number*; μυρίων ὅσων εἰς τὴν πόλιν ἐληλυθότων ἐθνῶν. *Dion.* l. 2. p. 86. *Ed. Huds.*

science

science got footing among them, "the philosophers, with which that country abounded, were divided into all possible sentiments concerning the most important points of speculation." And why should the enemies of Christianity bring that as an argument against *revealed*, which it is not unusual for them to produce in favour of *natural*, religion. "The variety, says [k] one, "and the altercation among them whetted the wits of *Greece*." "Reason, says [l] another, had fair play; politeness prevailed; learning and science flourished." Debate therefore, according to their principles, is the key to knowledge; it opens the mind, and enlarges the understanding: and our greatest adversaries must acknowledge, that controversies and schisms in the church have been attended with these happy consequences. This was foreseen by a pagan philosopher, [m] *Themistius*; who, in order to persuade the emperor *Valens* to moderate his persecution of those who were of different sentiments from himself, ingenuously tells him, that the

[k] *Collins.*   [l] *Shaftsbury on Enthus.*
[m] *Socrat.* l. 4. c. 32. *Sozom.* l. 6. c. 36.

disagree-

disagreement of opinions among the Christians was but inconsiderable, if compared with that which obtained among the Greeks; praying him withal to consider, that the most excellent and useful arts, nay philosophy itself, the mother of all good arts, had risen from small beginnings; and would never have arrived to such an height of perfection, but by the difference of judgement and strife among artists and philosophers.

What was the state of learning, when men, basely submitting to the yoke of papal tyranny, durst not judge for themselves, but blindly embraced and implicitly followed every doctrine proposed to them by their spiritual guides? Ignorance and error usurped the seats of knowledge and truth, idolatry and superstition the altars of religion and piety. But when the Christian world, weary of the usurpation of *Rome*, began to canvass the tenets of religion, learning revived, and enabled its votaries to detect and expose the corruptions with which truth had been long obscured and disgraced: for true religion and learning

ing have always gone hand in hand; the same rays of intellectual light have constantly dispersed the clouds of ignorance and error. Contentions about the sense of scripture introduced the study of it in the original, and this occasioned a cultivation of the learned languages; which amply repaid literature for the assistances which religion had borrowed from it. It is to divisions in the church that we owe those inestimable treasures of divine knowledge, the writings of the apostles, and those of the ancient fathers, whose learning and good sense render them well worthy the attention of every scholar. To them we are indebted for the revival of literature among us, for the invaluable works of our first reformers and their successors, both against the papists and the numerous separatists from our communion; writings, which prejudice itself cannot rank below any human composition whatsoever. God " suffered his holy apostle *Thomas* to doubt for the more confirmation of the faith:" and for the same purpose has he permitted other Christians to doubt, that the truth might be more carefully examined, and

more

more firmly established: and that its professors being, after a diligent and accurate discussion, rationally settled in their belief, might become more honest and sincere in their profession. To heresies, nay to infidelity itself, the whole Christian world is obliged for those lasting provisions heretofore made in this country for the defence of religion: to them is owing the present institution; which it is to be hoped will, through the blessing of God on the abilities of those who succeed me, answer the pious and generous design of its author, promote the honour of this seat of learning, advance true religion, and effectually secure the bulwarks of Christianity against the secret artifices of its concealed, and the open attacks of its declared enemies.

It is objected to us, that our disputes with one another make convulsions in governments, and involve neighbourhoods in feuds and animosities; whereas [n] among the pagans different notions never disturbed the civil government; and the philoso-

---

[n] See *Collins*, ubi supra.

phers themselves, though they wrote in behalf of their several opposite sentiments, have not left a book behind them written with the least spirit of rancour or malignity. We will not at present controvert the latter part of the assertion: but with regard to the former, let it be observed, that the argument lies against the professor, not the profession. Christianity, so far from encouraging virulence, every where inculcates meekness and charity, and bids us º *put away all bitterness, and wrath, and anger, and clamour, and evil speaking, with all malice.* Yet this forbearance is not to degenerate into coldness and indifference; we are exhorted to ᵖ *contend earnestly for the faith once delivered to the saints.* Errors, however multiplied among believers, are no proofs against the truth of religion; but zeal and fervor in dispute is an argument of the sincerity of the contending parties, and of the dignity and importance of the thing contended for. Where a dispute appears light and trivial, a matter of curiosity and mere speculation,

---

º *Ephes.* iv. 31.   ᵖ *Jude* 3.

it is easy to debate with civility, and make the dispute a diversion and entertainment: but when men are persuaded that the cause they have undertaken is the cause of truth, the cause of God, and that their eternal welfare is intimately and necessarily connected with it, zeal will naturally and insensibly hurry the meekest into indiscretion, those of a warm temper into violence and acrimony; who through fear of betraying, too often by their conduct dishonour, that truth which by their reasonings they defend and confirm.

[q] The name of Christian is common to every sect which professes Christianity, as that of philosopher is to every one who pretends to study philosophy: and therefore the different opinions, the errors, and absurdities of Christians ought not to be charged to Christianity, any more than the different opinions, errors, and absurdities

---

[q] This argument is made use of by *Justin Martyr* in his *Apology* to *Antoninus Pius*; where he takes notice of many blasphemous heresies which were, to the great scandal of Christianity, even then maintained. *Apol. ad Ant.* p. 53. *Ed. Oxon.*

of philosophers to philosophy itself. They depend upon and proceed from the determination of our minds and wills, which God has not thought fit to over-rule in the oeconomy of the church, any more than in the moral government of the world. What reason can be assigned, why God should exert his almighty power in restraining [r] *Diotrephes who loved the pre-eminence* in the church from *ecclesiastical*, any more than other ambitious men who love pre-eminence in the state from *secular* rebellion? All human societies are subject to intestine differences and commotions; armies to mutinies, kingdoms to rebellions; because the members of which they are composed are naturally subject to those passions from whence mutinies and rebellions arise; and for the same reason the church must necessarily be exposed to similar inconveniencies as the body politic: which however are in both attended with this *eventual* advantage, that by that means good subjects are distinguished from the bad, sincere and faithful Christians from the unsteady and hypocritical.

[r] 3 *John* 9.

SERMON VI.

The different opinions which have at all times obtained in the church are a direct and full confutation of that foul aspersion cast upon us by our adversaries, that a Christian is in his belief merely passive: they are a proof that the doctrines of our religion are examined, sifted, and canvassed by its professors; that they make use of their understanding; and, though like other men liable to prejudices, do not give their assent without consulting that reason with which God has for this purpose endued every man.

The necessity of defending our holy faith against modern infidels, and its particular doctrines against the corruptions and perversions of modern heretics, has caused Christianity to be viewed in every light; every part of it to be more clearly explained, and the whole better understood than it was or possibly could be in those ages, when a servile attachment to prescribed opinions kept the intellectual faculties of mankind in a state of perpetual stagnation. To these advantages the divisions which obtained in the primitive church have greatly

greatly contributed, by furnishing us with a most conclusive argument for the *authenticity*, as well as by being made an instrument of preserving the *purity* of the sacred oracles. [s] " So firmly, says *Irenæus*, are the gospels established, that the heretics themselves bear testimony to them, each of them endeavouring to confirm his tenets by their authority." This put them all as well as the orthodox upon their guard, and made them vigilant against the corruptions and interpolations of opposite sects. And thus to *heresies* it is under the providence of God owing, that the records of the Christian faith have been transmitted down to us without any material alteration: the suspicions and jealousies of Christians of all denominations being constantly kept awake; especially in the early ages, when any innovations attempted to be introduced in scripture could immediately

---

[s] Tanta est autem circa hæc evangelia firmitas, ut et ipsi hæretici testimonium reddant eis, et ex ipsis egrediens unusquisque eorum conetur suam confirmare doctrinam. — Quando ergo hi qui contradicunt nobis testimonium perhibeant et utantur his, firma et vera est nostra de illis ostensio. *Iren. adv. hær.* l. 3. c. 11.

(whilst the originals were yet extant) be by collation detected and confuted.

These are the *eventual* advantages arising from heresies and schisms: were these wanting, yet ought they not to stagger our faith, or induce us to doubt of any of the doctrines of our religion. The writings of the Evangelists and Apostles abound with exhortations to unity and concord; the spirit of Christianity breathes nothing but love, peace, and charity: Yet the author of our religion, by his prophetic spirit, declared that he was ᵗ *not come to give peace on earth, but rather division.* The doctrines of Christianity are laid down in scripture with a plainness and perspicuity sufficient and satisfactory to every well-disposed mind: yet we are every where cautioned against *false doctrines* and *false prophets* who were to arise, against ᵘ *men of corrupt minds, who raise perverse disputings.* These disputings and divisions in a religion, whose doctrines and precepts are so averse to them, are surely proofs of the divine

ᵗ *Luke* xii. 51.   ᵘ 1 *Tim.* vi. 4, 5.

inspiration

inspiration of those who foretold them; and therefore so far from being an objection against their religion, they are on the contrary a strong confirmation of its truth and divine original. And as such they are adduced by [w] *Justin* the Martyr against *Trypho: For that very reason,* says he, (*because there are such men who profess themselves Christians, and acknowledge the crucified Jesus to be their Lord and Christ, yet do not teach his doctrines, but those of the spirits of seduction*) *we who follow the true and pure doctrine of Jesus Christ are thereby confirmed in our faith, and in the hope revealed by him.* For what he by his prescience foretold should be done in his name, those very things we see with our own eyes actually accomplished. He then quotes several passages, wherein our Saviour foretells *divisions* and *offences,* and warns his disciples against [x] *false Christs and false prophets; which coming in sheep's clothing, but being inwardly ravening wolves, should deceive many; nay if it was possible the very elect.* To these might easily be added

[w] *Dial.* p. 100. *Ed. Jebb.*
[x] *Matth.* vii. 15. *Matth.* xxiv. 11. 24.

a very large catalogue from the writings of the apostles; which abound with predictions of heresies, and forewarn us of great corruptions of the faith, and in particular of one solemn defection and apostacy, which was to [y] "overspread the visible face of "the catholic church of *Christ*, and eclipse "the light of Christian verity and belief." *There shall be false teachers among you,* says St. *Peter, who shall bring in damnable heresies, even denying the Lord who bought them.* [z] *The spirit,* says St. *Paul, speaketh expressly, that in the latter times some shall depart from the faith, giving heed to seducing spirits and doctrines of devils — forbidding to marry, and commanding to abstain from meats,* &c.

This last prediction naturally puts us in mind of that church, the members of which (as we have observed before) on account of the many sects and divisions amongst us, and their great pretended unity among themselves, fallaciously conclude, and often persuade men of weak understandings, that *our* church cannot be,

[y] Mr. *Mede*'s *Discourse* on 2 *Pet.* ii. 1.
[z] 1 *Tim.* iv. 1.

but

but that *theirs* muſt be and is, the true church.

Neither variety of opinions, nor even diviſions and ſchiſms, can be an argument againſt the truth and catholicity of *any* church, for this plain reaſon—becauſe they are, in the nature of things, incident to *all* churches: and ſurely nothing can be concluded from a common affection of all churches againſt any particular church, any more than againſt an individual from a misfortune common to all mankind. When our Saviour was told of ᵃ *the Galileans, whoſe blood Pilate mingled with their ſacrifices; he ſaid, Suppoſe ye that theſe Galileans were ſinners above all Galileans, becauſe they ſuffered ſuch things? I tell you nay.* We muſt not intrude into the councils of providence, and judge of perſons by God's viſible diſpenſations towards them, but by their converſation towards God: and in the like manner we ought not to paſs a ſentence of condemnation upon a church, becauſe of God's preſent viſitation of it in

ᵃ *Luke* xiii. 1, &c.

the heresies and schisms of some of its members, but on the contrary form our judgement of it by the faith which it professes, the doctrines which it teaches, and the manner in which *Christ* is worshipped, and his sacraments administred. [b] *It has been declared*, says St. *Paul* to the *Corinthians, that there be contentions among you.*—*Every one of you saith, I am of Paul, and I of Apollos, and I of Cephas, and I of Christ.* Some of them despised his apostolical authority; nay some denied the resurrection, which is a fundamental article of the Christian faith: yet notwithstanding these schisms and heresies, and the scandalous vices of *particular* persons found among them, he salutes in both his Epistles the church in general by the title of *the church of God.*

It is union in one general interest which constitutes the very idea of a community; and communities formed upon bad principles and for bad purposes oftentimes agreeing better among themselves than the good and holy, *unity* alone cannot be an

[b] 1 *Cor.* i. 11, 12.

absolute distinguishing character of the truth. ^c The schismatical *Israelites*, who formed a separation under *Corah*, were as firmly connected as those who preserved their allegiance to *Moses* and *Aaron*; neither were the two tribes, which served the true God at *Jerusalem*, more at unity among themselves than the ten others in the false worship at *Bethel:* yet this very union was criminal in the sight of God, and therefore brought upon both societies those dreadful punishments that are recorded in holy writ. Where do we read of such perfect unity and agreement as in that ^d apostate congregation, when both people and high-priest joined in making the golden calf, rearing an altar before it, offering sacrifices, dedicating a solemn festival in its honour, and shouting without one dissentient voice — *These be thy Gods, O Israel, which brought thee out of the land of Egypt?* Nevertheless did this perfect concord and unanimity recommend or justify their defection? It was a confederacy in rebellion and apostacy; and therefore would have been their utter destruction,

^c *Numb.* xvi. ^d *Exod.* xxii.

had

had not *Moses* by his intercession turned God from his wrathful indignation.

At what period was the Christian world more united, than when *Constantius* and [e] *Valens* by their persecutions and cruelties had almost extirpated the *Nicene faith*, and established *Arianism* over the whole empire; when truth was confined to the deserts, and error reigned triumphant in the habitable provinces and the metropolis of the world?

Union is an ornament to a *good* cause, but no argument in favour of a *bad* one. If a church is no longer to be accounted true and catholic than whilst the members of which it is composed are unanimous, what shall we say in defence of the primi-

---

[e] *Valens* ordered at one stroke eighty ecclesiastics (who were deputed by the catholics to lay before him their grievances and the violence of the *Arians*) to be put to death. They were all put on board one vessel; which was set on fire at some distance from the land by the mariners, who saved themselves in the boat. The vessel with those that were left in it was entirely consumed. *Socrat.* l. 4. c. 16. The historian adds, that this barbarity did not escape the vengeance of heaven, but was punished by a dreadful famine. See *Univ. Hist.* T. XVI. p. 333.

SERMON VI. 219

tive church; which, as we have seen before, was from the very beginning rent asunder by heresies and schisms? What will the church of *Rome* say for itself, when ^f *Novatianus*, one of her own presbyters, raised a schism in the midst of her which soon grew into a perfect separation? When ^g *Liberius* subscribed to the sentence of the *Arian* bishops, and joined communion with those who granted to *Constantius* the title of *eternity*, which they denied to the *Son of God*? Where was its boasted union, when on the death of *Liberius* two different persons, *Ursinus* and *Damasus*, were elected bishops of *Rome*; part of the clergy and people adhering to one and part to the other, ^h with violent animosities and blood-

---

^f *Novatius*, a priest of *Carthage*, who had caused a schism there against *Cyprian* being then at *Rome* joined *Novatianus*. They are often confounded. This schism happened in the year 252. See *Euseb. Hist. Eccl.* l. 9. c. 43.

^g *Liberius* was made bishop of *Rome* in the year 352. *Ammianus* in the 15th book of his history tells us, that *Constantius* actually took the title of *eternal*: and *Athanasius* reproaches the *Arians* with acknowledging it. Περὶ τȣ̂ κυρίȣ προσποιούμενοι γράφειν ἄλλον δεσπότην ὀνομάζȣσιν ἑαυτοῖς Κωνστάντιον· αὐτὸς γὰ̓ ἦν ὁ τὴν δυναστείαν τῆς ἀσεβείας αὐτοῖς παρέχων· καὶ αἰώνιον δὲ αὐτὸν βασιλέα εἰρήκασιν, οἱ τὸν υἱὸν ἀΐδιον ἀρνούμενοι. *Athanas. de Synod.*

^h *Ammianus Marcellinus* tells us, that the prætor *Vicentius* was obliged to quit the town, and mentions as a certain

fact,

shed on both sides? When, to ascend somewhat higher, in the time of *Zephyrinus*, [1] *Natalis* the confessor having through vanity and avarice embraced the heresy of *Theodotus* was the occasion and the head of a schismatical separation, being made bishop by the heretics, and receiving from them a monthly salary? Let this pretended pattern of union and concord, this boasted center of Christendom, recollect the bitter and fierce contentions that have been among its members about *the deposing power, the personal infallibility of the pope, the authority of general councils, the immaculate conception,* and various other doctrines; *Thomists, Scotists, Occamists; Dominicans, Franciscans, Jansenists, Molinists,* and *Jesuits,* all against each other; nay council against council, and pope against pope. Let them recollect *schisms,* not proceeding from different doctrines, but of a far more

---

fact, that there were no less than 137 persons killed in the church in one day.—Constat in basilica Sicinini, ubi ritus Christiani est conventiculum, uno die centum triginta septem reperta cadavera peremptorum. *Amm. Marcell.* l. 27.

[1] This happened about the year 206. *Natalis* afterwards acknowledged his fault, and was admitted again into the bosom of the church. *Euseb. Ecc. Hist.* l. 5. c. 28.

scandalous nature, betwixt several pretenders to the chair of St. *Peter*; each of whom, with an equal arrogance and the same claim to infallibility, thundered forth his anathemas against his competitors and all their adherents. Let them, I say, recollect all this; and then, if unity must be the ordeal of a true church, let them assume and appropriate that name to themselves.

It is not bare *unity*, but the object and the cause of the union; it is unity in the true doctrine, in the true worship, and in the true administration of the sacraments; it is holding *the communion of saints* that makes a church truly catholic and apostolical; and therefore though the sectaries and heretics in this nation were infinitely more numerous than they are; yet while the *Church of England* continues to preserve within itself that unity which we have just now described, those that adhere to its doctrine and worship, however inconsiderable in kind or number, must notwithstanding constitute a truly catholic and apostolic church. We have every essential

sential character of unity with the catholic church of *Christ*, [k] *one Lord, one faith, one baptism*. We acknowledge and pay obedience to the same *head* of the whole Christian church, not *an earthly bishop*, but our Lord *Jesus Christ*. We have unity with it in the profession of the same *faith and doctrine*, not founded on the authority of *man*, but of *God* — that common [l] *faith once delivered to the saints*, and contained in the holy scriptures. We are at unity with it in the *administration* and *participation of the sacraments* according to *Christ*'s own institution and the apostolical practice. [m] *By one spirit we are all baptized in one body.* [n] *We being many are one bread and one body, for we are all partakers of that one bread.* [o] *We are all made to drink into one spirit.* These are the essential marks and characters of Christianity; which marks whatever particular church maintains inviolate,

---

[k] *Ephes.* iv. 5. Una nobis et illis fides, unus Deus, idem Christus, eadem spes, eadem lavacri sacramenta: semel dixerim *Una Ecclesia sumus. Tertull. de Virg.* Nam cum Dominus unus atque idem sit, qui habitat in nobis, conjungit ubique et copulat suos vinculo unitatis. *Firmil.* apud *Cypr. Ep.* 75.
[l] *Jude* 3.   [m] 1 *Cor.* xii. 13.
[n] 1 *Cor.* x. 17.   [o] 1 *Cor.* xii. 13.

maintains unity with the catholic church: on the contrary, whatever church departs from any of these departs from catholic unity, and consequently those that separate from such a church prove themselves to be true Christians, by departing from error, idolatry, and superstition; they maintain and manifest their adherence to and communion with the catholic church of *Christ*; they obey the commands of God — [p] *Come out of her, my people, that ye be not partakers of her sins, and that ye receive not her plagues.*

As it is our duty to separate from those who depart from the true faith and worship of Christ, so are we on the other hand indispensibly bound to maintain catholic unity; firmly to adhere to, and on no account withdraw from, the communion of those who preserve the doctrines and institutions of our Saviour and his Apostles. Every act of communion with such a *particular* church is a virtual communion with the whole *catholic* church

[p] *Revel.* xviii. 4.

diffusive; and consequently ⁴ a separation from it is a virtual separation from the catholic church; it is a renunciation of concord and correspondence with all men and all societies of men professing the same faith, and paying the same obedience to the laws enjoined by *Christ* and his disciples: which is the true Christian notion of schism, and constitutes its guilt. ⁵ *It must needs be,* says St. *Matthew,* ἀνάγκη ἐςι *there is a necessity* (not a *proper and absolute* but a *conditional* necessity) *that offences should come;* considering the state of the world (which is a state of probation) the freedom of man's will, and the frailty of his nature, it is *morally impossible,* or, as St. *Luke* explains St. *Matthew,* ⁶ ἀνένδεκ[όν ἐςι it is not to be expected *but that offences must come:* but such a necessity as this, arising entirely from the perverseness and wickedness of man, does by no means extenuate guilt, or excuse him who in any measure or degree contributes to this evil: for it is added, *Wo to the man by whom the offence*

⁴ Ὁ τὴν πρὸς ἡμᾶς κοινωνίαν ἀποδιδρᾴσκων μὴ λανθανίτω ὑμῶν τὴν ἀκρίβειαν πάσης ἑαυτὸν τῆς ἐκκλησίας ἀπορρηγνύς. *Baſ. Ep.*75.   ⁵ *Matt.* xviii. 7.   ⁶ *Luke* xvii. 1.

cometh.

cometh. As by *herefies* the good fo likewife the bad are made manifeſt; by herefies *publicly and obſtinately maintained*; for herefy confidered as a private opinion kept fecret within the breaſt of the perfon who holds it, however dangerous to himfelf, cannot be productive of thofe mifchiefs which the apoſtle complains of. By *herefies* he means falfe doctrines publicly and obſtinately maintained; by which animofities and ſtrife, divifions and fchifms, are introduced into the church; the weak are fcandalized, and the unwary feduced; religion expofed to contempt, and the truth of God to reproach.

To effect this his purpofe, the enemy of mankind has never failed finding proper inſtruments among the ignorant, the vain, the ambitious, and the contentious. When churches indeed are guilty of fuperſtition and idolatry, or any other corruption either in faith or practice; fo far from endeavouring or wifhing to difunite them by diverfities of opinions, he will by all poffible means ſtrengthen the bands of their union in his intereſt, keep them firmly and ſteadily

steadily attached to their corruptions. On the contrary, the nearer a church approaches in its doctrine and worship to ancient and primitive purity, the more he exerts every nerve, and employs all his subtilty and malignity to weaken and disgrace it by contentions and divisions, if not against faith yet against charity. For what faction and rebellion are in the state, that schism and separation are in the church; and therefore God allows of none but what are necessary: they are destructive of all peace and order, and tend to the confusion and bane of Christian fellowship and charity, to the decay and ruin of Christian piety. Men may talk of love and mutual forbearance; but whilst altar is set up against altar and church against church, it is morally impossible but there must be animosities and envyings, reproaches and contempt to the advancement of the common enemy, and the weakening of the common cause.

These particulars — the heinous sin of schism, ' the author and promoter of it, its

---

' *Ignatius* in his epistle to the *Trallesians* bids them beware of separation and divisions as *the snares of the devil*;
he

mischievous effects, the disgrace and detriment it brings on Christianity in general—these particulars every true Christian cannot but wish were seriously considered by those, who being originally engaged in the same cause with us have withdrawn themselves from our communion; that they would lay to heart the woful consequences of these unhappy divisions, and cease to rend the seamless coat of *Christ*, lest together with it they tear his body also; that they would peruse with attention and without prejudice not only the writings of our own, but those of ᵘ foreign divines; those of some of the most eminent

---

he advises the *Ephesians* to meet often together and receive the sacrament in peace and unanimity, as the only method to weaken the *powers* of *Satan*, and prevent the ruin he would otherwise bring upon them by division. Indeed all the ecclesiastical writers constantly ascribe heresies and schisms to the craft and artifice of the Devil. It was, I conceive, in allusion to this that *Polycarp* called *Marcion* the eldest son of the Devil.

ᵘ Their opinion may be seen in *Durell, Cember, Falkner,* &c. It is worthy of observation that the many thousands, all *Calvinists*, who came over to this kingdom from *France* on account of their religion, joined communion with the *Church of England*, not with the *Dissenters*; though the laws of the land left them their free choice and liberty.

[w] among themselves concerning the *doctrine*, the *worship*, and the *ministry* of the church of *England*. If they would do this, I am persuaded that the most sober among them would return, and heal the wounds which they have made; they would find that the scruples which have been raised in their minds do not concern the fundamentals and essentials of religion, and therefore cannot justify a separation: they would find that the terms of our communion are lawful; they would return and [x] *have fellowship with us; and truly our fellowship is with the Father, and with his Son Jesus Christ.*

If scruples however about mere accidents and circumstances should induce any one, [y] contrary to the judgement and usage of

---

[w] See *The Case of Lay-Communion* by Dr. *Williams*.

[x] 1 *John* i. 3.

[y] *Eusebius* having given an account of different rites and observances in the eastern and western churches adds that, notwithstanding that diversity, they maintained unity and communion: οὐδὲν ἔλαττον πάντες οὗτοι εἰρήνευσάν τε, καὶ εἰρηνεύομεν πρὸς ἀλλήλους· καὶ ἡ διαφωνία τῆς νηστείας τὴν ὁμοιοσίαν τῆς πίστεως συνίστησι. When *Polycarp* came to *Rome* in the time of *Anicetus*; though there was a difference of opinion between them, yet they saluted each other with the kiss of charity: and though neither would give up his opinion,

yet

the primitive church, to break the unity of communion; let them not tempt him to break the unity of benevolence and charity. Let not zeal for purity be thought a sufficient plea for spiritual pride and intolerance; for railing accusations against those from whom he differs; for bitter invectives against institutions which tend to decency, order, and edification; for odious reflections on a form of worship which reason and scripture approve; for those foul reproaches of superstition and papistical corruption, with which how unjustly we are charged the common enemy found to his cost, when the church of *England* towards the close of the last century stood alone in the gap, and stemmed the torrent of popery rushing in and ready to overwhelm the land.

Of the truly Christian spirit of forbearance and charity let *us* set the example;

---

yet they received the *Eucharist* together; *Anicetus* in his own church yielding up out of respect the consecration of the elements to *Polycarp*; after which they departed in peace. This history, he adds, *Irenæus* recorded, and recommended for the peace and union of the church. *Euseb. Ec. H.* l. 5. c. 24.

let us endeavour to reclaim those, who have separated from us, with zeal but with temper. Mutual revilings widen the breach and shut up all avenues to conviction; if these were once open and prejudices removed, the voice of truth would soon be heard, the altars set up in opposition to the altar at *Jerusalem* be pulled down by those that raised them, and the ^z *city* be once more *at unity in itself:* then ^a *would Jacob rejoice and Israel would be glad;* and the enemies of our holy religion (fully convinced by our concord and unity that ^c*the kingdom of God is righteousness, and peace, and joy in the Holy Ghost*) would likewise *follow after the things which make for peace,* ^d *be like-minded one towards another according to Christ Jesus,* and together with us *with one mind and one mouth glorify God, even the Father of our Lord Jesus Christ.*

^z *Ps.* cxxii. 3.
^b 1 *Cor.* xiv. 25.
^d *Rom.* xv. 5, 6.
^a *Ps.* xiv. 7.
^c *Rom.* xiv. 17.

[This subject was very fully and ably discussed by several eminent divines during the *Popish Controversy,* and particularly by the learned Dr. *Hickes.*]

SERMON VII.

2 PET. i. 19.

We have also a more sure word of prophecy, whereunto ye do well that ye take heed.

WE have seen in the foregoing discourse how punctually our Saviour's prediction of the sad estate of the primitive church was fulfilled; how it was infested with heresies and schisms, even during the days of the Apostles, to whom [a] *God bore witness with signs and wonders, and divers miracles, and gifts of the Holy Ghost.* God had for wise reasons, some of which we have attempted to explain, permitted these

[a] *Heb.* ii. 4.

diforders to moleft it: yet did he not totally abandon it, nor fuffer the faithful ftewards of his myfteries to be entirely unfuccefsful: many that had been feduced were reclaimed by their labours, the wavering fettled, and the true believers confirmed in the faith. It cannot therefore but be highly ufeful for us to enquire into the fteps taken by thefe unerring guides; that we may be able on fimilar occafions to follow the directions of thefe wife counfellors, the advice and the precepts which by the conduct and affiftance of the holy fpirit are delivered down in their writings for our admonition, as rules and precedents for Chriftians of all fucceeding generations.

The Epiftle out of which my text is taken, was evidently written with a view of preferving the Jewifh converts from being feduced by [b] *falfe prophets and falfe teachers*, who among other damnable herefies *even denied the Lord that bought them.* It abounds with warm exhortations and

[b] 2 *Pet.* ii. 1.

powerful

powerful arguments against all doctrines destructive of the true faith; yet the advice which I just now read to you is ushered in with a very peculiar encomium above them all, and in a particular manner recommended by the Apostle to the attention of his disciples. He had urged to them the truth of their belief from that glorious testimony given to our Saviour at his transfiguration by God himself, *when there came such a voice to him from the excellent glory, This is my beloved Son in whom I am well pleased: and this voice,* says St. Peter, *which came from heaven we heard when we were with him in the mount.* This was undoubtedly a strong and convincing proof: yet he adds, *We have also a more sure word of prophecy,* or (as the passage might perhaps be better rendered) *But we hold,* or esteem, *the word of prophecy to be surer, whereunto ye do well that ye take heed.*

But what is meant by the *word of prophecy,* which is here so much extolled? for

---

c *2 Pet.* i. 17, 18.   d V. 19.

various

^e^ various have been the expositions given of it, and consequently of the argument which the Apostle is supposed to make use of. I shall not trouble you with a recital of them; but without farther preface propose and endeavour to establish what I conceive to be the real meaning of the text, and then add some few observations upon it.

By the *word* of *prophecy* in St. *Peter* I understand the *spirit* or *gift* of prophecy; as by the ^f^ *word* of *wisdom* and the *word* of *knowledge* in St. *Paul* are understood the *gifts* of supernatural wisdom and knowledge; gifts which, I apprehend, differ no otherwise from that of prophecy than parts from the whole. That this gift was then plentifully vouchsafed to the church we are well assured from many passages in the holy scriptures: and the persons favoured with it stand high in the catalogue of church-governors given us by St. *Paul*, ^g^ being ranked next to the *apostles* and be-

---

^e^ See Bishop *Sherlock*'s Discourses on Prophecy.
^f^ 1 *Cor.* xii. 8.   ^g^ 1 *Cor.* xii. 28. *Ephes.* iv. 11.

fore the *evangelists* themselves. When he lays open to the *Corinthians* the storehouse of God's graces, he scruples not to prefer prophecy to all other spiritual gifts; and the reason is, [h] *because he that prophesieth edifieth the church*. Hence may be gathered the nature of the *gift* and the *office* of a prophet. The *gift* was, as he explains it himself, [i] *understanding all mysteries and all knowledge*; the *office*, to make use of this gift for the instruction of the church. [k] For, though there be no doubt but prophets were endowed with the gift of foreknowledge, and did actually foretel future and contingent events, as a proof of their divine mission; yet are they in general represented to us as persons inspired by im-

---

[h] 1 *Cor.* xiv. 4.   [i] 1 *Cor.* xiii. 2.
[k] The word *prophet*, besides its grammatical import, viz. *one who foretells future events*, signifies likewise in the scripture language *a revealer of the will of God*. In this sense *Abraham* is stiled a *prophet*, and so is *John the Baptist*; though we read of no *predictions* made by either of them. This sense the word plainly bears when it is said *Exod.* vii. 1. *I have made thee* a God *to Pharaoh, and Aaron thy brother shall be thy* prophet; i. e. the revealer of what thou the God of *Pharaoh* shalt say to him; nor does it ever signify to expound or interpret scripture otherwise than by a *divine afflatus* or *gift of prophecy*. *Whitby* on *Luke* i. 57.

mediate

mediate revelation with an extraordinary measure of wisdom, for the understanding and explaining of the evangelical and mystical sense of the law and the prophets, that the infant churches might be instructed in the mysteries of the gospel, and confirmed into all truth. To this our Apostle refers, when he says that *no prophecy of the scripture is of private interpretation;* i.e. the exposition which the prophet gives of scripture is not his own private sentiment, it comes not from his own private suggestion, but from inspiration: [m] *for prophecy came not ποτε at any time, by the will of man, but holy men of God spake as they were moved by the Holy Ghost.* To these unerring guides the Apostle refers his converts, who were as yet but babes in Christ; and when he does so, it is plain that it is to the scriptures themselves that he ultimately refers them; and these he recommends as likely to produce a clearer and stronger persuasion, as a firmer bulwark against apostacy and errors, than even his own attestation of Christ's glorious

---

[m] 2 *Pet.* i. 20, 21.

transfiguration, when a voice from heaven declared him to be the Messiah.

Whether the evidence of *prophecy* be absolutely and in itself greater than the evidence of *miracles*, seems by no means to be (as some have imagined) the subject of the Apostle's argument. In the particular case before us he could not, I imagine, with prudence insist, or indeed lay any great stress upon the sole authority of *miracles*. The very persons against whom he wrote, though they contradicted his doctrine, pretended the influence of the same spirit, the same commission from heaven. The mystery of iniquity had already began to work; [n] false prophets, according to our blessed Saviour's prediction, had arisen, who were per-

---

[n] Such was *Simon Magus*, who not only *bewitched the Samaritans so with his sorceries that they all gave heed to him*, *Acts* viii. 9, 10. but in many places prevailed upon the people to worship him. Such were those whom St. *Paul* compares to *Jamnes* and *Jambres* the celebrated magicians of *Egypt*, 2 *Tim*. iii. 8. with many others mentioned not only by ecclesiastical writers, but also by *Josephus* the Jewish historian. *De bell. Jud.* l. 2. c. 23.

mitted

mitted to perform strange and wonderful things : ° *they came,* says St. *Paul, after the working of Satan with all power, and signs, and lying wonders.* When revelation was thus opposed to revelation, and both claimed to have the same character of truth stamped upon its doctrines by *miracles,* something surely besides miracles must be appealed to, to judge between them.

Why then does the apostle mention any supernatural occurrence at all? Why this of the transfiguration in particular, of which there were only *three* witnesses?

ᵖ There was a tradition in the earliest

° 2 *Thess.* ii. 9.

ᵖ *Euseb. hist. eccles.* l. 2. c. 1. Though Eusebius mentions only these *three* Apostles, yet *Clemens of Alexandria* (whom the historian quotes) adds St. *Paul* in the *first* and in the *sixth* book of his *Miscellanies*. This great Apostle had been called in an extraordinary manner to the ministerial office by God himself, and received the doctrines which he taught by immediate revelation from *Jesus Christ*. It is therefore not to be wondered at that heretics sheltered themselves under his authority, and pleaded private tradition from him for doctrines unknown to Christians in general, as well as from the *three pillars of the church,* whom our Saviour had chosen to be witnesses of that supernatural manifestation of his glory when God declared him to be his only beloved Son.

ages

ages of Christianity, that our blessed Saviour had more particularly instructed his three principal disciples, *Peter*, *James*, and *John* (those three who were present at the transfiguration) and taught them secretly and separately from the rest the mystical sense of the scriptures; that this science was by them communicated to the other apostles, from whom the Seventy and some few others received it; but that it was never committed to writing, these hidden mysteries being reserved for the perfect. What an opening was here made for heresies and schisms, whilst the minds of believers were as yet unsettled and liable to be [q] *carried away by every wind of doctrine?* The veneration in which oral tradition was held by the *Pharisees*, the Jewish *cabbala* and mysterious literature (which was then much in vogue) paved an easy way for the introduction of all these kinds of theology among the converts of that nation. The plain literal sense of scripture, not at all times easily accommodated to hypotheses, was soon abandoned; crude

[q] *Ephes.* iv. 14.

alle-

allegories and mythological fancies were substituted in the room of it, and false blasphemous doctrines grafted on the word of God, under pretext of the holy spirit, by wicked impostors of all denominations; [r] each of whom claimed, as partaker of this tradition, the knowledge of mysteries and an exclusive right of interpreting the holy oracles. Thus [s] *Basilides* in particular, who introduced among his many heretical opinions some of the Egyptian ἀπόρρητα into the Christian religion, boasted of having received his mystical science from *Glaucias* a disciple of St. *Peter*. Now if we suppose (and I cannot see any objection to the supposition; if we suppose, I say) that this tradition took its rise from those three disciples having received so eminent a mark of *Christ*'s favour, we cannot be at a loss for a reason, why our Apostle should, upon making mention of the transfiguration, appeal to another cri-

[r] *Moris erat gnosticis* (says the learned *Mosheim*) *qui divinos Christianorum libros ab opinionibus suis dissentire non poterant diffiteri, arcanos Jesu Christi et amicorum ejus sermones testari.*

[s] *Clem. Alex. Strom.* l. 7. p. 898. *Ed. Pott.*

terion for the truth of his doctrine.
[t] Satan and his emissaries (whose policy it always was to counterfeit the seal of the spirit of God) had already seized, or the Apostle foresaw that they would soon seize, hold of that respect and reverence with which men necessarily receive whatever bears the character of divine authority; and ushered into the world their impious and blasphemous doctrines under the specious title of a secret revelation vouchsafed to so distinguished an Apostle. To obviate the evil consequences of such a belief, he

---

[t] That this method of quoting the Apostles, for doctrines contrary to those which they taught, was practised even during their lifetime, may with some probability be conjectured from a passage in St. *Paul's second Epistle to the Thessalonians*, c. ii. *Now we beseech you brethren—that ye be not soon shaken in mind or be troubled, neither by spirit, nor by word, nor by letter*, as from us—and likewise from the conclusion. *The salutation of Paul with mine own hand, which is* the token *in every epistle:* the *token* undoubtedly of its being *genuine*, in opposition to *forged ones*, which had been obtruded upon them as his by some of these impostors. We find that, soon after his death, his name was made use of to gain credit to one of the most dangerous heresies that ever infested the church. *Valentinus* (from whom was derived one branch of the *gnostics*) was said by his followers, if we may credit *Clemens of Alexandria*, to have received his occult science from *Theodades*, who had been a disciple of St. *Paul*.

now introduces this supernatural manifestation of *Christ*'s glory on purpose, as it were, to depreciate his own authority, and inform them of another foundation on which they might rest their faith with greater security; even the invariable rule of truth, the head and fountain of all divine knowledge, the holy scriptures. But as ^u *cunningly devised fables* (σεσοφισμενοι μύθοι allegorical and mythological doctrines) were extracted from them by the false interpretations of the *gnostics* and other pretenders to superior knowledge; he appeals to their genuine meaning, as expounded by those whom the unerring Spirit of God had endowed with extraordinary wisdom and knowledge, ^w *for the perfecting of the saints, for the work of the ministry, for the edifying of the body of Christ; till they all come in the unity of the faith, and of the knowledge of the Son of God, unto a perfect man, unto the measure of the stature of the*

---

^u 2 *Pet.* i. 16.

^w *Ephes.* iv. 12, 13. That *to be perfect* in the scripture language signifies to be instructed in the Christian faith Dr. *Whitby* has, I think, clearly proved in his annotations on this passage and on 1 *Cor.* ii. 6.

fulness

fulness of Christ. What follows my text in St. *Peter* is clearly of the same import with this passage of St. *Paul*; and, as I apprehend, fully justifies the interpretation which I have put upon it. He exhorts his converts to *take heed to the word of prophecy, as a light that shineth in a dark place, until the day dawned, and the day-star arose in their hearts*; that is — until they were sufficiently instructed in the will of God, and arrived to a more perfect knowledge of all the articles of the Christian faith. Till that period came, the gift of *prophecy* constantly resided in the church; but when the mysteries of the gospel had been fully revealed it was gradually withdrawn, and at last totally ceased: the writings of the *New Testament*, which contain a more perfect light, being added to those of the *Old*, the church stood no longer in need of extraordinary assistance: but every Christian might read and understand the will of God clearly revealed in the holy scriptures: in which the sacred interpreters of the will of God, ˣ *though they be dead, yet speak:* the

---

ˣ *Heb.* xi. 4.

law and the *prophets* are explained by the gospel; *Moses* and *Elias* are seen (not by *three* only, as in that glorious vision referred to by St. *Peter*, but) by every true believer conferring with *Christ*.

Though the advice given by the Apostle primarily relates to the persons whom he more immediately addresses, and is adapted to their particular situation; yet is the duty recommended of general and perpetual obligation, of equal use and moment to every Christian of every age; for the truth upon which it rests is this—that the *scriptures are the only rule of faith*, the sole and infallible judge in all doubts and controversies. To them St. *Peter* refers us as well as the believers of his time, and (if I am not much mistaken) in opposition to both miracles and tradition which his successors have presumed to set up against them. But, thanks be to God, our faith [y] *is built upon the foundation of the apostles and the prophets, Jesus Christ himself being the chief corner-stone*. For where is the

[y] *Ephes.* ii. 20.

certainty

certainty of divine faith if it depends on other than divine authority? Truth is constant and permanent, and muſt therefore have a fixed and immutable baſis. The ſenſes are treacherous, memory unfaithful, reaſon fallible, philoſophy uncertain; but *[z] the word of our God ſhall ſtand for ever.* *[a] Salvation*, ſays our Saviour, *is of the Jews*; doubtleſs becauſe *[b] to them were committed the oracles of God*, the ſcriptures of the Old Teſtament, which contained the prophecies and promiſes of the *Meſſiah*. If ſuch was the privilege attending the records of the *old* covenant, how great muſt be the excellency of thoſe which furniſh us with a clear revelation of the *new* covenant, which is a full and final perfection of the old? *[c] If that which is done away was glorious, much more that* which remaineth is glorious.

Without entering into the diſpute, how far [d] miracles of themſelves, and unattend-

---

[z] *Iſ.* lx.   [a] *John* 4. 22.
[b] *Rom.* iii. 2.   [c] 2 *Cor.* iii. 11.
[d] See a *diſcourſe* in the popiſh controverſy *concerning the teſtimony of miracles* prefixed to a tranſlation of *the School of the Euchariſt*.

ed with any other circumstance, are to be admitted as proofs of the authority of any revelation, I scruple not to apply what St. *Paul* affirms of the gift of tongues to every other outward miraculous work — viz. ᵉ that *they are a sign not to them that believe, but to them that believe not*. Miracles are undoubtedly a most powerful testimony: while other arguments work their way by slow degrees, they make an immediate impression, and overwhelm, as it were, the mind with their evidence. They are therefore principally calculated

---

ᵉ 1 *Cor.* xiv. 22. See St. *Chrysostom Tom.* V. *Hom.* 88. the title of which is διὰ τί σημεῖα νῦν ἐ γίνεται, *why miracles are not wrought now. These things*, says Pope *Gregory* the first, *were necessary in the beginning of the church; for in order that the number of believers might encrease, faith needed to be nourished by miracles; in the same manner do we deal with young trees; we water them till they have thoroughly taken root, and then the watering ceases.* Greg. in Evang. Homil. 39. And yet this very pope was one of the greatest retailers of false and ridiculous miracles that ever disgraced Christianity. Very remarkable likewise is the following passage from the famous Jesuit *Acosta*. *Miracles are given to unbelievers, and the scriptures to those that believe; therefore the primitive church abounded in miracles, because unbelievers were to be called. But the church of latter times will trust more to scripture than to miracles, because believers are already called. Nay, I will say boldly that all miracles are vain and useless if they are not approved by scripture;* i. e. *if they have not a doctrine conformable to scripture.* Accost. de temp. noviss. l. 2. c. 19. See likewise the *second Nicene Council*, *Act*. 4.

for

for producing great and sudden revolutions and introducing new dispensations: they are necessary credentials to warrant the prophet's mission; because they command irresistibly our attention to the doctrines which he preaches, the faith which he proposes. When that end is attained, the law promulged, and the authority of the lawgiver established, the *necessity* nay the *use* of miracles ceases; and other means more suitable to our nature supply their place. A free use of our intellectual powers, and a sober diligent enquiry into the nature, extent, and meaning of the laws will procure a full satisfaction of all doubts, and an entire persuasion of the truth of any particular doctrine. For God having been pleased to make us rational creatures requires of us rational obedience; and therefore does not in the *ordinary* course of things supersede the exercise of those glorious faculties which, as they render us justly answerable for the sin of infidelity against satisfactory evidence, so likewise do they stamp a value upon, give a comeliness and beauty to even our faith. Our Saviour himself does not rest the divine

vine demonstration of the gospel entirely upon miracles, but often appeals to the scriptures as ᶠ *testifying of him* and *having the words of eternal life.* The apostles followed their Lord's example, and reasoned to the Jews out of the scriptures, confirming their doctrines from the books of the Old Testament. ᵍ And it is recorded of their immediate successors, men likewise endowed with the power of working miracles, that they were particularly careful, after they had laid the foundation of the faith, to deliver to their converts the holy gospel in writing. To these sacred records the ancient fathers of the church constantly appeal in all their doubts and disputes with heretics. ʰ *Let them,* says St. *Austin* speaking of the *Donatists, prove their church,*

ᶠ *John* v. 39.
ᵍ *Euseb. Hist. Ecc.* 3. 37. The apostles (says *Theophylact*) wrote the *gospels* ἵνα ἐκ τούτων διδασκόμενοι τὴν ἀλήθειαν μὴ παρασυρῶμεν ὑπὸ τοῦ ψεύδους τῶν αἱρέσεων, &c. that we learning the truth *from them* might not be perverted by the falshood of heresy, &c. *Theoph. Proem. in Matth.* The apostles, says *Irenæus,* first preached the gospel, et postea per dei voluntatem in scripturis nobis tradiderunt fundamentum et columnam fidei nostræ futurum, afterwards delivered to us in the scriptures what was to be the ground and pillar of our faith. *Iren.* l. 3. c. 1.
ʰ *August. de unit.* c. 18.

not by deceitful signs and wonders, but out of the law and the prophets, out of the word of Christ himself, out of the works of the evangelists, out of the books of scripture whose authority is canonical. Either, says he afterwards with respect to the miracles pretended to have been wrought by some of them; *either there is no truth in what is reported, or if they have really performed any thing miraculous, the more ought we to be upon our guard; because our Saviour (after having told us that deceivers shall arise who with signs and wonders shall, if it were possible, deceive the very elect) adds, recommending it with vehemence,* " Behold I told you be-" fore." These passages from one under whose authority the patrons of miracles so often endeavour to shelter themselves might, one would imagine, check their petulance when they insolently call upon us to produce miracles in proof of our doctrines, and their arrogance when they presumptuously claim an exclusive right to the title and benefits of a church on account of [i] *the glory,* as they term it, *of* their

---

[i] This is the eleventh out of fifteen notes by which the famous Cardinal *Bellarmin* pretends to find out the true catholic

pretended *miracles*. The holy scriptures are a fair copy of God's will declared by *Christ* and his apostles, God himself confirming their declaration [k] *by divine miracles and gifts of the Holy Ghost:* and the authenticity of this copy is proved beyond all doubt by the uniform concurrent testimony of all intermediate ages. Whoever therefore have again recourse to the evidence of miracles for the credibility of any of the doctrines of Christianity, require an additional seal to what God has already ratified; they depreciate his testimony, and render all his promises of none effect. This the *Romanists* must allow to be their case, or contend that their doctrines are new, or mission extraordinary. If their *mission* is extraordinary, it is not derived from the apostles with whom *Christ* promised to be [l] *always, even unto the end of the world:* and if their *doctrines* are new, we only say with St. *Paul,* [m] *If any man or angel preach another gospel,* than that which

---

catholic and infallible church; all of which he takes care to appropriate to the church of *Rome* only.
[k] *Heb.* ii. 4.   [l] *Matt.* xxviii. 20.
[m] *Gal.* i. 8.

SERMON VII.

Chriſt and his apoſtles preached, *let him be accurſed.*

But if *miracles* fail, the *Romaniſts* have another reſource; there are, if you believe them, unwritten ⁿ *traditions* preſerved in the church: into theſe all faith is reſolved, and every Chriſtian is enjoined to hold them (whenever the church pleaſes to produce them) in equal eſteem and veneration with the ſcriptures themſelves.

We have already obſerved on the authority of the primitive writers, that the true faith was firſt corrupted by perſons, who pretended to a more perfect knowledge of the doctrines of Chriſtianity tranſmitted by *oral tradition* from *Chriſt* and his apoſtles.

ⁿ This verity and diſcipline is contained in the written word and in the *unwritten traditions* of the fathers — reverencing all the books as well of the Old as New Teſtament, of both which God is the immediate author; as alſo the *traditions* themſelves, belonging both to *faith* and manners, dictated as it were from the mouth of *Chriſt,* or of the holy ſpirit, and *preſerved in the catholic church in a continual ſucceſſion.*—— If any one reading over theſe books—in the old vulgar *Latin* edition, does not hold them for *ſacred* and *canonical*; and knowing the *before-ſpecified traditions* does induſtriouſly contemn them, let him be *anathema* or accurſed. Counc. *of Trent, Seſſion* 4.

Now

Now if *tradition* perverted the truth so near the times in which the apostles lived, nay perhaps whilst some of them were still living; how can we expect that it should at this distance secure us from error? Let us only look back to the earliest ages of the world, when the want of writing made the use of tradition necessary, and the long lives of men rendered it less liable to accidents. What will history inform us but that error is almost coeval with truth? Religion committed to the care of so untrusty a guardian soon degenerated into superstition and idolatry; the law of nature was scarce written on the heart of man, but the characters became illegible. God therefore, when he chose to himself a peculiar people, engraved with his own finger the laws which he gave them upon two tables, and commanded them to be kept with religious care, that the people might have recourse to them upon all occasions. °*To the law and to the testimony*, saith God himself through the mouth of his prophet *Isaiah*, when the people were in danger of

° *Isaiah* viii. 10.

being

being seduced into idolatry. And in the time of general corruption what did the good *Josiah* do? [p] *He read in the ears of the people the words of the book of the covenant, and he made a covenant before the Lord to perform the words of the covenant that were written in this book.*

We know indeed that traditionary rites and customs obtained much at last in the Jewish church: but does not our Saviour say, [q] *in vain do they worship me, teaching for doctrines the commandments of men: for laying aside the commandment of God ye hold the tradition of men?* It is the appointment of God which constitutes a rule of faith: and can it enter into the heart of man to conceive that our Saviour would appoint that in *his* church, which he condemns in the *Jewish?* As the gospel was not to be confined within the narrow bounds of *Judea* but propagated all over the earth, it was in greater danger of being corrupted by oral tradition, and consequently stood in greater need of being secured by writ-

[p] 2 *Kings* ii. 3.   [q] *Mark* vii. 7, 8.

ing,

ing, and committed to the keeping of every Christian, as a standing and public record of the will of God and his own duty. And who that has such a record well authenticated would trust to ʳ vague and uncertain report? For why should the evangelists or apostles omit any essential doctrine, any article necessary for the belief of a Christian? It could not be out of *ignorance*, even putting blasphemy out of the question; because the traditions, which are supposed to contain these doctrines and these articles, are likewise supposed to proceed originally from them. To charge them with doing it *knowingly* is to charge them with partiality, with malice, with sacrilege; with the same sacrilege that the church of *Rome* is guilty of, when by depriving her members of the use of the scriptures she ˢ *takes away the key of knowledge, and* ᵗ *shuts up the kingdom of heaven against men.* It is moreover giving them the lie,

---

ʳ Τὰ γὰρ ἀγράφως λεγόμενα πάντα μετ' ὀλίγον οὐκ ἔχοντα ἀπόδειξιν; *For those things which are spoken without being committed to writing are of short duration, because they have no certainty.* Origen. Dial. cont. Marc.

ˢ *Luke* ii. 52.   ᵗ *Matt.* xxiii. 13.

since

SERMON VII.

since they every where profess that they make known to us *the whole gospel of Christ*, the whole counsel of God.

But supposing there were any such *apostolical traditions* as are pretended; they are acknowledged to have been delivered secretly and privately, and designed for the instruction of a chosen few: if so, then they were not intended for public use, and of consequence not necessary to be publicly known; if they were not necessary to be publicly known, they could not be essential to faith, and therefore cannot be imposed upon us as fundamental articles of our religion.

St. *Paul* tells us that " *the holy scriptures are able to make us wise unto salvation:* St. *James* that " *God begat us with the word of truth:* St. *Peter* that ˣ *we were born again not of corruptible seed but of incorruptible* by the word of God *which liveth and abideth for ever.* Yet we have been told that

" 2 *Tim.* iii. 15.   ʷ *Jam.* i. 18.
ˣ 1 *Pet.* i. 23.

it

it is "[y] a dead letter, capable of different
"meanings, according to the difference of
"time, accommodating itself to the hu-
"mours and maxims of the church;" that
"[z] to receive it as the only rule of faith is
"the foundation of atheism and impiety;"
that "it is the church which gives it all
"its authority and weight," and that
"without the church it would not merit
"more credit than the Fables of *Esop* or
"the Alcoran of *Mahomet*."

While we wonder at the absurdity and
abhor the profaneness of tenets like these,
we cannot without ingratitude omit our
thanks to the Almighty for the benefits
we enjoy in the communion of a church,
which not only rests its belief on the doctrines contained in the holy scriptures,
but likewise allows every member of it

---

[y] *Cusan. ad Boh.* Ep. 2.   [z] *Bellarm. de verb. Dei.* iv. 4.
Who can read these and other like passages without calling to mind the account which *Irenæus* gives us of the heretics of his time? Cum ex scripturis arguuntur in accusa-
tionem convertuntur ipsarum scripturarum, quasi non recte
habeant, neque sunt ex authoritate, et quia varie sunt dictæ,
et quia non posset ex his inveniri veritas ab his qui nesciunt
traditionem: non enim per literas traditam illam, sed per
vivam vocem. *Iren.* l. 3. c. 2.

free

free access to the laws of his Saviour, whose *words are spirit and life.* To lay a restraint upon the use of them is in itself so absurd and irrational, so manifestly contradictory to God's great purpose of revealing his will to all men; that it is justly matter of the highest admiration, as well as indignation, that any Christian church could be guilty of and justify such an enormity, under pretence of preventing mischiefs which must arise from the reading of them.

That some parts of scripture are obscure and difficult to be understood we deny not; and that [b] *the unlearned and unstable wrest them to their own destruction* we likewise acknowledge. It is what St. *Peter* himself complained of, and yet he did not forbid the use of them: he knew that they were *holy, just,* and *good;* and therefore if " men (whose curiosity is above their
" faith, whose affectation of singularity
" above the care of their souls) will search
" the scriptures to find out new doctrines,

[a] *John* vi. 63.   [b] 2 *Pet.* iii. 16.

" and

"and if they cannot find them will bring them thither;" the fault lies not in the scriptures, but in their own rashness and presumption: they are, says St. *Paul*, *'proud, knowing nothing, but doting about questions and disputes about words, whereof cometh envy, strife, evil surmisings, perverse disputings of men of corrupt minds, and destitute of the truth.* But to argue from *abuse* to *non-use* is not logical. The perversion of scripture cannot with propriety be charged upon scripture itself; especially when it proceeds, as it generally does, from ignorance, pride, prejudice, or interest. For let a passage be never so express, and the sense common and obvious; yet, if the doctrine contained in it militates against the prepossessions of a zealot, some other meaning must at all events be contrived, and the words (though written with ink made of light) tortured till they are at last obliged to comply with the principles of the interpreter.

'1 *Tim.* vi. 4, 5.

To prevent or cure these disorders, our adversaries pretend that there is in their church an *infallible judge* appointed by God himself. The apostles were, if any men can be, infallible judges; yet there were in their time (as their own writings fully prove) as many controversies and differences about matters of faith, as many and as great heresies and schisms, as have been since in any age of the church. *Infallibility* therefore is no certain remedy against them: but suppose it were, where are we now to find it? for, though the *Romanists* boast much of having this infallibility among them; yet where it is lodged, whether in the *pope alone*, or in a *general council alone*; or in the *pope and council concurring*, or lastly in the *church diffusive*, are points in which they are not yet agreed; and truly (as has often been observed) no great stress can be laid upon the infallibility of that church, that does not itself know where its infallibility resides.

The doctrines of Christianity are of two kinds, the *moral* and the *mystical*. These last may likewise be divided into two classes. The *first* class consists of what St. *Paul* calls [d] *the principles of the doctrine of Christ*, the rudiments and groundwork of faith, the fundamentals of our religion, the articles contained in the Creed. The *second* class is made up of truths important indeed but not so obvious; such as the wonderful dispensations of God towards the amazing work of our redemption, his eternal purpose even before the world began, his gradual revelations to the patriarchs, the types, prophecies, and various prefigurations of the *Messiah* in the legal worship, the calling in of the Gentiles upon the rejection of the Jews, and the future glorious state of the church when, upon God's calling again his chosen people, [e] *the Gentiles shall come to their light, and kings to the brightness of their rising*—These, I say, and others of the like sublime and abstruse nature, form the second order of *mystical* doctrines. Now rightly to appre-

[d] *Heb.* vi. 1.   [e] *Is.* lx. 3.

hend and reap benefit from these requiring more study, a greater use and improvement of reason, a sounder judgement, and a more enlarged understanding than God has thought proper to endow every man with; they are therefore (though highly ornamental of the Christian character) not of absolute, indispensible, universal necessity. But the *moral* and the first class of the *mystical* doctrines, being absolutely necessary to the very being of a Christian, are therefore delivered without obscurity or ambiguity, are plain and evident to all, even persons of the meanest capacity. " *Theo-*" *logy* is the profession of a few, *religion* " the duty of all."

What shall we say then of those sublime objects of the catholic faith, those divine mysteries which are confessedly above the reach of all human understanding? Is not the belief of them of absolute and indispensible necessity? Undoubtedly it is; and therefore are they, like all the other doctrines contained in the first class, expressly and positively revealed; and (though their nature

nature and relations are utterly inconceivable by human reason, yet) to the truth of them, because they are confirmed by the testimony of God, human reason itself cannot but give a firm, full, and immediate assent. For " truth being a confor-
" mity to the nature and reason of things,
" the word of him who spake all things
" into being cannot but be infallible
" truth." But is the book of *nature* full of mysteries, and shall we wonder at a few in the book of *grace?* '*Thine own things, says the angel to Esdras, and such as are grown up with thee canst thou not know; how should thy vessel then be able to comprehend the way of the highest?* If sensible things are above our reach, shall we repine because we cannot grasp those that are invisible? Let us rather bless God for what he has been pleased to reveal clearly, and what reason cannot fathom let faith contemplate. For though it be utterly impossible that any revelation from God can be contradictory to reason, for then

' 2 *Esd.* iv. 10, 11.

truth would be at variance with truth; yet it is very possible that there may be truths in that revelation, to the clear perception and full comprehension of which our faculties are not proportioned; [g] *that our faith may not stand in the wisdom of man, but the power of God.* And however the pride of man may recoil at the thought of a truth inconceivable by him, yet sober reason will readily acknowledge and adore the wisdom and the goodness of God in proposing mysteries for the trial of our faith, as well as precepts for the exercise of our obedience. They command our attention and veneration; they teach us to set a due value on the means of grace, to have a just sense of our imperfections and the all-sufficiency of God. Humility and piety are twin-sisters, offspring of that [h] *wisdom which is from above.* The man that cherishes these Christian graces cannot but be highly favoured by the divine principle which produced them; heavenly truths

---

[g] 1 *Cor.* ii. 5.   [h] *James* iii. 17.

meeting with no obstruction in their passage to his mind strike with full force, and make a deep and lasting impression. Such a man as this; a man (who with a becoming awe and reverence enquires into that good, perfect, and acceptable will of God) finds new truths continually emerging, and beaming out their light upon his understanding: while he converses in the book of God, he converses with and is partaker of all the privileges and revelations of the Prophets, Evangelists, and Apostles; he converses with God himself: God, by the ministry of his word, speaks to him from heaven; he speaks to his heart and soul such comfort and invincible demonstration, as all the pride of learning and philosophy can never attain to.

Thus does the true Christian begin here upon earth an intercourse and communion with God, and enjoys through the gospel a foretaste of that marvellous light, which will be the portion of the saints in bliss; when grace being perfected in glory, ry, we shall view more nearly the [i] *mystery hid from ages*, the stupendous work of our redemption, the wonders of God's nature, the riches of his goodness, and the treasures of his mercy. [k] *Now we see through a glass darkly, but then face to face: now we know in part, but then we shall know even as we are known.*

[i] *Col.* i. 26. [k] 1 *Cor.* xiii. 12.

SERMON VIII.

Phil. iv. 8.

Finally, brethren, whatsoever things are true, whatsoever things are honest, whatsoever things are just, whatsoever things are pure, whatsoever things are lovely, whatsoever things are of good report; if there be any virtue, and if there be any praise, think on these things.

IT is observed of St. *Paul* that, however obscure and irregular his argumentation may sometimes appear to those who want either abilities or attention to trace the connexion of the several parts of which it is composed, yet his general method in all his epistles is plainly regular and easily
per-

perceptible to every understanding. Having given a solemn testimony of his affection by recommending the churches to the peace of God, he begins his discourses with *doctrinal* and ends them with *moral* precepts; having first grounded and settled his flock in the true faith, he then proceeds to recommend a practice suitable to that faith.

It has been my aim and sincere endeavour to follow the example of this blessed Apostle: and, having accordingly in my former discourses treated of the chief fundamental points contained in the speculative part of our holy religion, I now purpose, by God's assistance, to recommend a conduct corresponding to our profession; to prove that not only the belief of *whatsoever things are true*, but likewise the practice of *whatsoever things are honest, just, and pure* is required of us as necessary to salvation.

The *intellectual* virtues indeed in point of order take place of the *moral* ones, because a rational agent acts in consequence
of

SERMON VIII.

of knowledge: for how, without the knowledge of our duty, can there be an established rule of our obedience? But though knowledge is thus essential to practice, yet is not practice the less necessary to knowledge. *[a] Who is a wise man, and endued with knowledge amongst you? let him shew out of a good conversation his works with meekness of wisdom.*

One of the many devices, made use of by the enemy of mankind, is to keep men in extremes of opinion with regard to matters of faith and doctrine: he [b] *transforms himself into an angel of light*; and, under the specious pretence of saving them from a dangerous error, hurries them away to the opposite precipice; passing over the intermediate space, where the saving and profitable truth is usually to be found at an equal distance from both extremes. Thus with respect to the doctrines now under consideration — A pernicious error was by his artifices introduced in the infancy of the church, by which men were taught to

---

[a] *James* iii. 13.   [b] 2 *Cor.* xi. 14.

believe

believe that *works alone without faith* were sufficient to justification and salvation: but, this heresy being confuted by apostolical arguments and authority, he very dexterously changed the question, and instilled into weak minds the more flattering poison of the opposite doctrine, persuading them that they might be justified *by faith alone without works:* whereas the scriptures join them both together, expresly teaching us that nothing availeth to salvation ᶜ *except faith which worketh by love*; i. e. a vigorous and operative faith productive of good works, a sincere obedience proceeding from a true and vital faith.

And first, that *works alone* are not sufficient to procure God's favour, he himself has clearly taught us in that comprehensive epitome of his laws, which he wrote with his own finger, and delivered by the ministry of his servant *Moses* to his chosen people. The commands of the *first* table immediately and solely respect his authority, and the obedience and worship which

ᶜ *Pal.* v. 6.

SERMON VIII.

is due to him: from whence this inference naturally follows, that our faith in him and obedience to his authority are the foundation of the moral commandments contained in the *second* table. This confideration greatly exalts and ennobles morality, interefting the Supreme Being in all our acts of virtue; which if they proceed from any other principle, inafmuch as they refpect not God, are at leaft a virtual difavowal of his authority. In all our actions as well as opinions are to be confidered what the fchoolmen call the *materiale* and the *formale*; not only the act itfelf, but the fundamental ground on which it refts, and on account of which it is performed. For it is not the fuperftructure that fupports the foundation, but the foundation that gives ftability to the fuperftructure: let the edifice be ever fo fplendid or ftrong in itfelf, yet (if the foundation be unfound) the whole building muft partake of the weaknefs upon which it relies. [d] There are many truths believed, the

---

[d] See this point argued with his ufual acutenefs and precifion by Dr. *Crackenthorp* in his *Vigilius dormitans*, c. 13.

scriptures themselves are received in the church of *Rome*; yet I am afraid that this belief and acknowledgement have very little of the nature of a true Christian faith; because, however true and commendable they are in themselves, they proceed from an antiscriptural principle: they depend upon the infallible authority of the pope enjoining them, a doctrine which is contrary to and subversive of faith. The case is the same with our outward actions: they may be good in themselves, but not in the agent; in them the will of God may be *performed*, but not *obeyed*: for there is a wide difference and easily perceivable between an act itself and the obedience observed in that act. Every moral virtue considered abstractedly is, without all doubt in the matter of it agreeable to the will of God; but it does not follow that the will of God is obeyed in the performance of every moral action. It may and too often does proceed from merely human principles, from custom, example, convenience, interest: and, as water will not rise higher than the level of the spring from which it flows, so neither can an act be better
than

than the motive from which it took its rise. Should we therefore allow it even the highest principle which a mere moral philosopher can claim, the *idea of the intrinsic beauty and loveliness of virtue;* yet even then, inasmuch as it wants the concurrence of that which God requires, and which reason itself properly exercised must teach us to be the principal duty in nature, i. e. *respect to his laws and submission to his authority*—wanting that principle it cannot recommend man to God's favour. It has indeed so far the nature of sin, that it is setting up the understanding of man against the knowledge of God: it is a renunciation of our allegiance to him, a contempt of those attributes of power, wisdom, goodness, and holiness, upon which his laws and our obedience to them are founded. [e] *Thou art worthy, O Lord, to receive glory, and honour, and power;* for *thou hast created all things, and for thy pleasure,* i. e. by thy will alone and divine command,

---

[e] *Rev.* iv. 11. Upon this principle it is that the *Roman philosopher* calls Piety *Justice towards God.* Est enim pietas justitia adversum deos. *Cic. de Nat. Deor.* l. 1.

and for the manifestation of thy glory, *they are, and were created.* How can God receive glory and honour from his creatures, but by their solemn acknowledgement of his supreme dominion and authority over them, and their entire dependence upon him? And how can they shew that acknowledgement but by constantly looking up to him with a filial fear and reverence, and by directing their actions out of conscience of their duty to him, making his will their motive, his laws their rule, and his glory their end. *If I be a father, where is mine honour?* *If you call him father, who without respect of persons judgeth according to every man's work, pass the time of your sojourning here in fear,* i. e. a reverential and godly fear, such as becometh *obedient children.*

Self-gratification and self-sufficiency were the cause of the first sin, and have ever since been the chief ingredients in all subsequent

---

f *Mal.* i. vi.   g 1 *Pet.* i. 17. *If you call him father who judgeth* — This certainly is the meaning of εἰ πατέρα ἐπικαλεῖσθε τὸν κρίνοντα, not, as our Version reads, *If you call upon the father who judgeth.*

SERMON VIII.

transgressions: nay, they have scarce ever failed to insinuate themselves in and pollute our best actions. This fatal prevalency of those two principles was the cause, why the [h] *Stoics* and *Epicureans* stood foremost in the list of those who opposed St. *Paul* preaching the gospel at *Athens:* he preached [l] *Christ crucified to the Greeks foolishness*; because his doctrine destroyed that *sensual self* which was the measure of the one, and disowned that *moral self* which was the foundation of the other philosophy. If our actions have respect only to ourselves, how can we expect that God will regard us, while we are thus regardless of him; that he will honour us while we seek honour from ourselves, and not [k] *the honour which cometh from God only?*

How far indeed God will accept or reject the moral virtue of those, who had not so exact a knowledge of him and of his will as we have been blessed with, would be presumptuous in us to attempt to deter-

[h] *Acts* xvii. 18.   [i] 1 *Cor.* i. 23.
[k] *John* v. 44.

mine. Thus much we may venture to assert, because it is expressly declared, that *God is rich to all that call upon him*; that *he is the God not of the Jews only, but also of the Gentiles*; that *he is no respecter of persons, but in every nation he that feareth him and worketh righteousness is accepted with him*; that *when the Gentiles, who have not the law, do by nature the things contained in the law; they having not the law are a law unto themselves.* Yet even here faith is by no means excluded; to works of righteousness is added the fear of God; and the observance of that natural law is required by which man, being capable of knowing God, was bound to honour him as God. However he may be pleased to deal with the gentile world, his declarations with regard to us are explicit. *Without faith it is impossible to please God.* As *the altar sanctifies the gift*, so does faith consecrate our actions rendering them *spiritual sacrifices acceptable to God by Jesus*

---

^l *Rom.* x. 12.   ^m *Rom.* iii. 29.
ⁿ *Acts* x. 34, 35.   ^o *Rom.* ii. 14.
^p *Heb.* xi. 6.   ^q *Exod.* xxix. 37.
^r 1 *Pet.* ii. 5.

Christ.

Chrift. ^s *By faith the elders,* all righteous men from the foundation of the world, *obtained a good report.* It was *faith* which recommended the sacrifice of *Abel* to God; while *Cain*'s offering and duty, which did not proceed from the same inward principle, were both rejected. For ^t *unto the pure all things are pure ; but to them which are defiled and unbelieving is nothing pure ; but even their mind and confcience is defiled.* All their actions (however good in appearance, whatever external conformity they may have to the letter of the law) are polluted by the infidelity of their hearts: for where the fountain is poifoned, all the streams iffuing from it partake of the infection. ^u By the Mofaical law, as a degree of holinefs was conveyed to every thing that touched what was dedicated to God's fervice, fo likewife legal impurity was contracted by the touch of any thing unclean: and this law of impurity is thus beautifully applied by the prophet *Haggai* —^w *If one touch any of thefe,* things holy,

---

^s *Heb.* xi. 2. 4.   ^t *Tit.* i. 15.
^u *Levit.* vi. 27.   ^w *Hag.* ii. 13, 14.

shall it be unclean? And the priest answered and said, it shall be unclean. Then answered Haggai and said, so is this people and so is this nation before me, saith the Lord; and so is every work of their hands, and that which they offer is unclean. ˟ The want of true faith and inward obedience to God's command (which they shewed by the manner in which they performed that very command) made all their actions, nay even the sacrifices which they offered on his altar, hateful and unacceptable.

A religious motive and reverence to the divine authority were esteemed by the Jews so essential to a good action, that it was a received maxim among them, that *he who obeys any command of God, but not in his*

˟ The building of the temple, which had been obstructed by the *Samaritans*, and totally stopped by an order from *Artaxerxes*, as the monarch then reigning is called by *Ezra*. Upon his death the *Jews* obtained a fresh decree from *Darius* his successor, and the work was resumed; but they shewed such backwardness and indolence in carrying it on, that God punished them with a great drought which blasted and withered all the fruits of the earth; a curse, as Mr. *Lowth* judiciously observes, formerly denounced against them for their disobedience. See *Levit.* xix. 24. *Deut.* xxviii. 23. compared with *Hag.* c. i.

name,

SERMON VIII.   279

name, shall receive no reward. The natural reasons of this maxim I have considered pretty largely; because it is a point in which many well disposed persons are very apt to mistake, the eyes of their minds being dazzled by the splendor of what are called philosophical principles: as if God required not the heart as well as the head; as if reason, while it is exalted by the contemplation of the nature and relations of things, was debased by the remembrance of him who constituted that nature and those relations. *^y Whatsoever ye do,* saith the scripture, *do all to the glory of God. ^z Whatsoever ye do in word or in deed, do all in the name of the Lord Jesus Christ. ^a Glorify God in your body and in your spirit which are God's.* God has an entire right over the whole of us by creation, preservation, and redemption. When therefore we withdraw any part of us from his service; when we make our own reason our supreme rule, ^b *going about to establish our own righteousness* instead of *submitting ourselves*

^y 1 *Cor.* x. 31.   ^z *Col.* iii. 17.
^a 1 *Cor.* vi. 20.   ^b *Rom.* x. 3.

S 4   *unto*

unto the righteousness of God, we invade his right, we rob him of what belongs to him not only by original propriety, but moreover by subsequent purchase. And this we are guilty of whenever we glorify him not in our *spirit* as well as our body; when our actions, though morally good, proceed not from spiritual principles and are not directed to a spiritual end. As such actions have no respect to God, we cannot expect him to delight in them; and what he does not delight in, he will not reward. The mystical union between *Christ* and his church is represented to us in scripture by the matrimonial union subsisting between a man and his wife: faith is the bond, and good works resulting from that faith the fruit of that union: all other fruits are out of wedlock, and consequently can have no right to the inheritance.

But *secondly*, though good works are not of themselves *sufficient*, yet are they *necessary* to salvation; though faith is *necessary*, yet it is not of itself sufficient.

When

SERMON VIII. 281

When *Satan* drew our first parents into disobedience, he very artfully began by instilling into their mind doubts concerning the command of God: [c] *Yea, hath God said ye shall not eat?* Having once raised scruples about the law, he boldly urged a total disbelief of the punishment annexed to the breach of it. [d] *Satan said, ye shall not surely die.* As *incredulity* paved the way to sin, so should *faith* introduce righteousness, and by *obedience* raise human nature to that state of excellence from which it was degraded by *disobedience*. We debase religion when we turn it into barren speculation; when we study the law of God merely out of a desire of knowledge, without attending to the practical excellencies with which it abounds; when we take delight in the bare act of knowing, and neglect the duties which ought to accompany that knowledge; forgetting that by the *good ground* in the parable of the sower our Saviour himself tells us are meant [e] *they,*

[c] *Gen.* iii. 1. [d] *Gen.* iii. 4.
[e] *Luke* viii. 15.

who

who not only hear the word, but *in an honeſt and good heart having heard it keep it, and bring forth fruit with patience.*

It is an acknowledged axiom among thoſe who believe any religion at all, that the firſt principle in religion is to endeavour *to imitate the deity.* It has its foundation in nature: both our affections and reaſon perſuade us to aim at attaining thoſe excellencies which we admire in others: even ſelf-love aſſiſts us in performing this duty. No perſon of any ſentiment can reflect on any advances, which his nature makes towards a ſimilitude to the moſt perfect of all beings, without the higheſt complacency and delight. This pleaſure is greatly encreaſed by the additional reflection, that he is fulfilling the end of his creation, and acquiring the friendſhip and favour of him whoſe favour and friendſhip is man's higheſt felicity and honour. [f] God cannot but behold with approbation

---

[f] Τίς τάξις φίλη κỳ ἀκόλυθθ- Θεῷ; μία, κỳ ἕνα ἔχυσα ἀρχαῖον λόγον, ὅτι τῷ ὁμοίῳ τὸ ὅμοιον φίλον ἂν εἴη. *Plat. de Leg.* l. 4. Ἐκείνυς προσδέχεθαὶ αὐτὸν δεδιδάγμεθα κỳ πεπείσμεθα κỳ πιστεύομδυ τὰς τὰ προσιόντα αὐτῷ ἀγαθὰ μιμουμδῥους, σωφροσύνην, κỳ δικαιοσύνην, κỳ φιλανθρωπίαν, κỳ ὅσα οἰκεῖα Θεῶ ἐςί.

in his rational creatures, every degree of conformity to that everlasting holiness and righteousness which, being essential to his nature, constantly and invariably determine his actions; and are therefore made the rule and the motive of theirs. With this view he created man in his own image. To renew this image, after it had been defaced by sin, has been the gracious purpose of all his dispensations. When he selected to himself a peculiar people, this was the general preface and introduction to the laws which he prescribed, ^g *ye shall be holy, for I the Lord your God am holy.* And this declaration of God's will is particularly applied by ^h St. *Peter* to the Christian religion; the true professors of which are said ⁱ *to have put on the new man, which is renewed after the image of him who created him;* ^k *which after God,* καΊὰ Θεὸν *after the similitude of God, is created in righteousness and true holiness.* For this purpose he sent down ^l *the express image of his person,*

^g *Levit.* xix. 2.   ^h 1 *Pet.* i. 16.
ⁱ *Coloss.* iii. 10.   ^k *Ephes.* iv. 24.
^l *Heb.* i. 2.

that we might have a *visible* pattern and example of those excellencies and perfections which we are required to imitate; that by the exercise of Christian virtues upon Christian principles we might [m] *be conformed to the image of the Son of God,* [n] *be made partakers of the divine nature,* and from a likeness to *Christ* in holiness now be made like unto him in glory hereafter.

As [o] *the Law was our School-master to bring us to Christ,* so is the Gospel our teacher by which we are trained up for the kingdom of heaven. The duties which it prescribes are not only a necessary *condition,* but moreover a necessary *qualification* for it. [p] *Nothing that defileth can in any wise enter into heaven.* Every impurity alienates the mind from God and from every thing that is spiritual and holy. How then can a soul defiled with sin be a fit companion for those spirits, who are ever employed in the contemplation and adoration of that holy

---

[m] *Rom.* viii. 29.
[o] *Gal.* iii. 24.
[n] *2 Pet.* i. 4.
[p] *Rev.* xxi. 27.

Being

Being who [q] *is of purer eyes than to behold iniquity?* Surely they are ill qualified to join with the blessed choir above, whose very [r] *prayers are an abomination unto the Lord:* they can be but ill-disposed to pay continual praises and thanksgivings to God, who have been always accustomed to disregard his attributes, despise his wisdom, reject his mercy, and hold his power and justice at defiance. There can be no pleasure where the object is not suited to the faculties that receive it: as therefore a carnal man can never delight in spiritual duties, nor he that is immersed in matter relish those that are altogether intellectual: so neither can the envious, the revengeful, and the malicious (without a miracle wrought in their favour) become capable subjects of that happiness which consists of peace and universal benevolence. For [s] *what fellowship hath righteousness with unrighteousness?* What communion or agreement can envy, malice, hatred, and revenge have with charity, goodness, and love?

---

[q] *Habac.* i. 13. [r] *Prov.* xxviii. 9.
[s] 2 *Cor.* vi. 14.

love? They are as opposite as darkness to light, as *Belial* to *Christ*. We must lay the foundation of our spiritual building on earth, if we mean to have it finished and perfected in heaven: we must perform good works in this world, if we wish to enjoy the reward belonging to them in the next.

When the lawyer asked our Saviour [t] *what he must do to inherit eternal life*, the only rule which he prescribed to him was *obedience*. *If thou wilt enter into life, keep the commandments.* Christianity does not exempt us from any moral duty. Some of the circumstances indeed of the moral law are abrogated; but its substance and authority still remain and will for ever remain in full force. [u] *It is easier for heaven and earth to pass than one tittle of the law to fail.* The same sins are forbidden, the same virtues required, the same duties recommended and enjoined in the gospel and in the law; but not on the same terms. The law considered as a covenant of works

[t] *Matt.* xix. 16, 17.   [u] *Luke* xvi. 17.

admitted

admitted of no mitigation : but under the gofpel, which is a covenant of grace, repentance reftores the tranfgreffor to the favour of God, and inftead of perfect exactnefs, the fincere endeavours of a true believer are through the merits of *Chrift* accepted.

But does not this diffolve our obligation to obedience? God forbid : on the contrary it makes the obligation ftricter. We are not only bound by the authority of God's injunction, but by the exprefs command of our Redeemer and Mediator ; we have a clearer knowledge of our duty, and the affiftance of the holy fpirit to perform it : we have better and more explicit promifes, and fuller affurances of reward. Every wilful tranfgreffion under fuch advantages acquires an additional degree of guilt ; and therefore our Saviour tells us that ʷ *except our righteoufnefs fhall exceed the righteoufnefs of the Scribes and Pharifees, we fhall in no wife enter into the kingdom of heaven.* They had refpect only to the *out-*

ʷ *Matt.* 5. xx.

ward

ward deed; whereas in a Christian *inward* intention and purity of heart are required: they made the applause of men and their own credit the principle and end of their actions; but to a true Christian the glory of God is the end; love, obedience, and faith in his promises the principles and motives of righteousness. Hence is Christian obedience stiled the [x] *work of faith and* the *labour of love*. Christian *faith* is a vital and operative habit of mind; it works powerfully upon every faculty, quickens every grace, and makes our obedience willing, easy, and constant. *Love* is a passion of the mind which excites us to action; it follows with pleasure, pursues with vigour, and promotes with unwearied application the interest and honour of its object: our affections are no sooner fixed upon any particular person, but our thoughts and desires are immediately eager and restless after opportunities of shewing our reverence and esteem; we study to please, we try all methods to oblige him, we receive his commands with pleasure, and

---

[x] 1 *Thess.* i. 3.

SERMON VIII.

we execute them with chearfulness. Every motive to love afforded by the gospel is likewise a motive for obedience. *If you love me keep my commandments.* As obedience without love is slavery; so love without obedience is but an abstracted, wild, and fruitless speculation, without any foundation in reason and the nature of things. For "what is rational *love*, but a *desire to pleaſe* the person beloved, and a *complacency* and satisfaction *in pleaſing him?* To love God therefore is to have a sincere *deſire of obeying his laws*, and *a delight* or pleasure *in the conſcience of that obedience.*" Men's practices are the best indexes of their principles. If the love of God was firmly rooted in the heart, it would soon shew its power and efficacy by springing up into action and abounding in every duty, in all goodness, and righteousness, and truth. And hence (because these two principles of *faith* and *love* are the main springs of all our good actions) our obedience by a figure of speech naming the cause alone, where together with it the

---
John xiv. 15.

T effect

effect is intended and underſtood—by this figure, I ſay, our obedience to the laws and commands of God are often in ſcripture expreſſed by our *faith* in him, our *love* of him, and by other cauſes and principles which produce or chiefly concur in producing that obedience. But if love and faith are the principal cauſes of good works; then ſurely Chriſtians, who have ſuch ſuperior motives to love God and have faith in him, are of courſe under greater obligations to a ſincere, conſtant, and univerſal obedience. Without that our love is hypocriſy, our faith nothing more than an hiſtorical or dogmatical belief, and ſo far from ſaving will condemn us. [z] *For if we ſin wilfully after that we have received the knowledge of the truth, there remaineth no more ſacrifice for ſins. He that deſpiſed Moſes's law died without mercy under two or three witneſſes. Of how much ſorer puniſhment, ſuppoſe ye, ſhall he be thought worthy, who hath trodden under foot the Son of God, and hath counted the blood of the covenant wherewith he was ſanctified an unholy thing,*

[z] *Heb.* x. 26. 28, 29.

SERMON VIII.

and hath done despight unto the spirit of grace?

The gospel is a covenant of mercy, and also a law of obedience. *Jesus Christ* is our Lord as well as Saviour: he came into the world to rescue us from the *dominion* as well as the *punishment* of sin; [a] *that we being delivered from our enemies might serve him without fear in holiness and righteousness all the days of our life.* [b] *He gave himself* (says St. *Paul*) *that he might redeem us from all iniquity.* It was by no means the design of *Christ* to tolerate the practice of sin, or abate men any part of their moral duty: on the contrary he has adopted and perfected the moral law; and having made it a standard and rule of obedience to himself he has, as lord and lawgiver, enjoined the strict observance of it, under the title of his commandments, to his disciples as an indispensible condition of eternal happiness. [c] *Christ is the author of eternal salvation unto all them,* and them only, *who*

[a] *Luke* i. 74.   [b] *Tit.* ii. 14.
[c] *Heb.* v. 9.

obey

obey him; who pay him an actual and positive obedience and service. ^d The man who *hid his talent in a napkin* was condemned for neglect of duty; not because he had squandered it away, but because he had not improved it. ^e The barren *fig-tree*, an emblem of those who content themselves with a bare profession, was cursed because it bore only leaves and no fruit; and ^f *every tree, which bringeth not forth good fruit, is hewn down and cast into the fire.* No human legislator ever discovered his mind more clearly and fully upon any subject than our divine legislator has upon this. ^g *Why call you me Lord, Lord, and do not the things which I say?* ^h *Not every one that saith unto me Lord, Lord, shall enter into the kingdom of heaven, but he that doeth the will of my father which is in heaven.* In the sketches which he has been pleased to give us of the great day of retribution, he every where tells us expressly that man shall be finally rewarded according to his works; that not only the

---

^d *Luke* xix. ^e *Matth.* xxi. 19.
^f *Matth.* iii. 2. ^g *Luke* vi. 46.
^h *Matth.* vii. 21.

mere

mere name of Christianity, and the naked profession of the faith without the practice of it, but even eminent and extraordinary gifts without obedience to his commands shall avail nothing to salvation. [i] *Many will say unto me in that day Lord, Lord, have we not prophesied in thy name, and in thy name cast out devils? and in thy name done many wonderful works? And then I will profess unto them, I never knew you; depart from me ye that work iniquity.* The same truth is upon all occasions declared to us by his embassadors. [k] *In them* only, according to St. *Paul, there is no condemnation; in them* only is *the righteousness of the law fulfilled, who walk not after the flesh but after the spirit;* they only *are the sons of God, who are led by the spirit of God.* [l] St. *James* wrote professedly in defence of this doctrine; and St. *John,* the beloved dis-

---

[i] *Matth.* vii. 22, 23.   [k] *Rom.* viii. 1. 4. 14.
[l] Many of the antients (and our most excellent Bishop *Bull* subscribes to their opinion) tell us that the contrary doctrine owed its rise to a misinterpretation of some passages in St. *Paul*; and that against this misinterpretation and the notion consequent upon it *the Epistle of St. James, the first of St. John, the second of St. Peter,* and that of *St. Jude* were written.

ciple of *Christ*, tells us that ᵐ *whoso keepeth his word, in him verily is the love of God perfected.* ⁿ *Let no man deceive you, he that doeth righteousness is righteous; whosoever doeth not righteousness is not of God.* And in another place, ᵒ *Blessed are they that do his commandments, that they may have right to the tree of life, and may enter through the gates into the new Jerusalem.*

The word which is here rendered by the *English* word *right* is ἐξουσία; which word, as every one who has the least acquaintance with the *Greek* language must know, signifies not an *absolute inherent* right, a right of *merit* (as the church of *Rome* insolently teaches) but only a right of *permission:* and therefore the passage ought to have been rendered, *that they may have liberty, may be permitted, to come to the tree of life.* In every claim of absolute right there must be an equivalence, a natural proportion between the work and the reward. Now what proportion can

ᵐ 1 *John* ii. 5.   ⁿ 1 *John* iii. 7. 10.
ᵒ *Revel.* xxii. 14.

there

there be between a *temporary* obedience and an *eternal* reward? Besides, our obedience at best is but imperfect: and were it perfect yet, as it is our bounden duty to God, it could not of right and justice challenge a reward from him to whom it was due. What title then, what right have they *that do God's commandments* to eternal life? I answer, a title *by promise*, a *stipulated federal* right. In every covenant there must be conditions; in the covenant made, through the mediation of *Christ*, between God and man the condition on the part of man is obedience to God's commands, and to this obedience God on his part has been pleased to annex the promise of eternal life; and therefore St. *Paul* calls the gospel [p] *the truth which is after godliness in hope of eternal life, which God that cannot lie promised.* The same veracity and faithfulness, which will most assuredly bestow the reward upon those who fulfil the conditions, is likewise bound to exclude those who neglect the terms of the covenant. To what purpose should

[p] *Tit.* i. 1, 2.

men be exhorted to ^q *bring forth fruits meet for repentance,* to ^r *live righteously soberly and devoutly,* to ^s *put on the whole armour of God,* to ^t *put on the new creature which is created after God in righteousness and true holiness,* if after all the *Son* was to extend his merits, and the *Father* accept them in favour of those who will do none of these things? Such a supposition would confound all notions of right and wrong, destroy all distinction between virtue and vice, and rob God of his truth, his justice, and his holiness — of his *truth*, since he has ^u *revealed his wrath against all ungodliness and unrighteousness of men who hold faith in unrighteousness,* and hath excluded all such from ^w *any inheritance in the kingdom of Christ and of God:* of his *justice* in giving the righteous man's reward to transgression and disobedience: of his *holiness*, for then ^x *the workers of iniquity would stand in his sight,* ^y *his eyes would behold evil and look on iniquity.*

^q *Matth.* iii. 8.
^s *Ephes.* vi. 11.
^u *Rom.* i. 18.
^x *Pſ.* v. 5.

^r *Tit.* ii. 12.
^t *Ephes.* iv. 24.
^w *Ephes.* v. 5.
^y *Habac.* i. 13.

I scarce

SERMON VIII.

I scarce need observe how much this doctrine of *the necessity of good works* has been controverted in almost every age of the church by *schoolmen* studious of perplexing clear passages with nice metaphysical subtilties and distinctions; by weak *ignorant* men fond of using scripture terms without understanding their meaning; and by warm *enthusiasts* who find mysteries in the plainest phrases, and then work themselves up into a belief that to them alone it is given to understand mysteries. What can be plainer, when not darkened by words without knowledge, than the true notion of our salvation by the grace of God? And yet how has it been misapplied, without any countenance whatever from scripture, to support the doctrine of *unconditional election and reprobation?* a doctrine so absurd that one may well wonder how it could find reception among philosophers, so impious that a sincere Christian can with difficulty conceive how it ever could prevail among divines: a doctrine destructive of the principles of our reasonable nature and of at least the moral part of divinity,

nity, and contradictory to every covenant which the wifdom and goodnefs of God has been pleafed to make with fallen man. *[z] Walk before me*, faid he to *Abraham, and be thou perfect; and I will make my covenant between me and thee.* If *Abraham* was not a free and rational agent capable of breaking as well as keeping this covenant, to what purpofe was it made? If his election was unconditional, why does God require conditions of him? And if there is no neceffity of faith and obedience, why are they made the exprefs conditions? Why is he fo highly commended in the fcriptures of the *New Teſtament*, and propofed as a pattern of faith and obedience to all Chriftians? When God afterwards made a covenant with the *Jews*, [a] *Moſes read the book of the covenant in the audience of the people; and they faid, All that the Lord hath faid we will do, and be obedient.* When *Joſhua* renewed it again, the people faid [b] *The Lord our God will we ſerve, and his voice will we obey.* Does it not from

[z] *Geneſ.* xvii. 1, 2.   [a] *Exod.* xxiv. 7.
[b] *Joſh.* xxiv. 24.

thefe

these promises and asseverations evidently follow that they were conscious of an elective principle within themselves; of faculties competent to act as well as intend, to perform as well as promise; of powers sufficient to denominate their good actions their own, and give their loyal obedience a title to the favour and protection of God? The same observation may be made of the covenant of grace; the many passages which I have cited, wherein good works are required of Christians, being a plain and full proof that as we are rational creatures capable of acting with design and counsel, so does God expect that by a proper use and application of our faculties that design and that counsel should be directed to his honour and glory, and to the performance of those conditions upon which he has made our salvation to depend.

The term *grace* (which has given occasion to this unseemly notion of justification without the use of any means whatsoever) implies kindness and favour, including in it the idea of a superior who freely and voluntarily

luntarily bestows that favour. Hence it is used in different significations and for different gifts, when applied to different persons and on different occasions; but when used in general without a reference to any particular instance, the *free grace of God* has only two significations. It means either that special act of his mere goodness whereby he was pleased, without any obligation on his part or claim on ours, to restore us to his favour through the satisfaction of a Redeemer: or it means that other act of undeserved mercy whereby God, for the sake of our Saviour and thro' the intervention of his merits, will accept of sincerity instead of perfection, of a hearty and honest instead of a sinless and unerring obedience. In the *first* sense we are said to be ^c *justified freely by his grace through the redemption that is in Jesus Christ*; and in the *latter* to be ^d *justified by grace, not of works*.

These are not the only passages out of the writings of St. *Paul* which have been

^c *Rom.* iii. 24.   ^d *Ephes.* ii. 8, 9.

made

made subservient to the introduction of dangerous errors concerning this important doctrine. He has said in several places that *e man is justified by faith without the deeds of the law:* and from hence many even learned men (without paying the least attention to the numberless other positive texts of scripture, and to the nature of that faith and those works which are here mentioned) have cried down the necessity of good works, and attributed the whole of our *justification* to *faith alone*; as if evangelical obedience was no part of the evangelical covenant; and men might in contradiction to the direct words of our Saviour *f enter into life* without keeping the commandments. The works which the apostle excludes from any share in our justification he himself calls in express terms *the deeds of the law:* for the right understanding of which it is necessary to observe that the converted *Jews* had brought into Christianity all their prejudices in favour of the *Mosaical* law, and urged the neces-

---

e *Rom.* iii. 28.—v. 1. *Gal.* ii. 16.—iii. 24.
f *Matt.* xix. 17.

sity of strictly adhering to all its rites and ceremonial performances. Against these patrons of *legal* servitude the apostle of the *Gentiles* every where asserts [s] *the liberty wherewith Christ hath set us free*; and, in order to set forth and vindicate the superior excellence and pre-eminence of the gospel, he strongly presses and inculcates the doctrine of *justification by faith in Jesus Christ*: i. e. by the *Evangelical* in opposition to the *Mosaical* dispensation. But he does not any where oppose faith to works of righteousness which are founded in *Christ*; he no where tells us that man is justified by a mere solitary belief; that an empty speculative faith, an assurance, a reliance and recumbence on *Christ*, that laying hold on the skirts of his garments and wrapping ourselves up with his righteousness will be sufficient to place us in the number of the righteous, and qualify us for the kingdom of heaven. Alas! this is not faith but folly, this is not hope but presumption. Why has God made us capable of moral influences, if we are not

[s] *Gal.* v. 1.

subject to moral duties? Why has he implanted such an active principle in us, and promised us the additional assistance of his holy spirit, if that principle is useless, that assistance unnecessary? Great things indeed are spoken of faith; but they are spoken of a true Christian faith; which is the cause and spring of Christian piety, which implies and includes within it the whole and entire condition of the gospel.

It is worthy of observation how careful St. *Paul* is, lest we should have any other notion of the faith which he so much extols. Does he tell the *Galatians* that [h] *in Jesus Christ neither circumcision availeth any thing, nor uncircumcision, but faith which worketh by love?* Lest his meaning though clearly enough expressed should notwithstanding be mistaken, he more fully explains himself in a parallel passage to the *Corinthians* — [i] *Circumcision is nothing, and uncircumcision is nothing; but the keeping of the commandments of God.* Is *Christ* in one

---

[h] *Gal.* v. 6.   [i] 1 *Cor.* vii. 19.

place stiled by him [k] *the Saviour of all especially those that believe?* he is in another called [l] *the author of eternal salvation unto all them that obey him.* He recommends and urges the practice of righteousness by every motive that can influence a Christian. Even in the midst of that discourse, on which the *solifidians* so much rely, he draws an argument in favour of good works from that very faith which is set up in opposition to them. [m] *We are buried with him by baptism into death; that, as Christ was raised up from the dead by the glory of the Father, even so we also should walk in newness of life.* As the bad lives of believers reflect dishonour upon God and his religion, so the best security of the honour of Christianity is a strict observance of its laws: he therefore exhorts us to shew ourselves [n] *patterns of good works, that he that is of a contrary part may be ashamed, having no evil thing to say of us — that we may adorn the doctrine of God our Saviour in all things—*[o] *that we may*

---

[k] 1 *Tim.* iv. 10. [l] *Heb.* v. 9.
[m] *Rom.* vi. 4. [n] *Tit.* ii. 7, 8. 10.
[o] *Phil.* ii. 15.

be

SERMON VIII.

be blameless and harmless, the sons of God, without rebuke. He presses them from their suitableness to the profession of Christianity, and (that powerful motive of obedience) the will of God. ᵖ *Let your conversation be as becometh the gospel of Christ.* ᑫ *Walk as the children of light (for the fruit of the spirit is in all goodness, and righteousness, and truth) proving what is acceptable unto the Lord.* ʳ *For this is the will of God even your sanctification.* They are our calling, the great end and design of the gospel revelation. ˢ *God hath not called us unto uncleanness but unto holiness.* ᵗ *This is a*

ᵖ Phil. i. 27.   ᑫ Ephes. v. 8, 9, 10.
ʳ 1 Thess. iv. 3.   ˢ 1 Thess. iv. 7.
ᵗ Tit. iii. 8. Two learned men, *Grotius* and Dr. *Hammond*, contend that St. *Paul* by his exhortation *to maintain good works* means no more than that Christians should follow some honest labour and vocation. This opinion the latter endeavours to establish by remarking that the word ἐργάζεσθαι is always used by the apostle to signify bodily labour: but as ἐργάζεσθαι is not the term made use of in this passage; this criticism, however true, cannot prove what is intended by it. The apostle had in the foregoing verses spoken of our justification by the *free grace* and mercy of God in *Jesus Christ*. Lest therefore this doctrine should be abused, he here immediately gives a strict and solemn charge to *Titus* to press the necessity of *good works* upon all those who embrace the gospel. The conclusion drawn by the two great men before mentioned does by no means correspond with the premises. Can any one seriously imagine that St. *Paul* would in so solemn a manner usher in

U   a matter

faithful saying, and these things I will that thou affirm constantly that they, which have believed in God, might be careful to maintain good works. ᵘ *Our Saviour Jesus Christ gave himself for us that he might redeem us from all iniquity, and purify unto himself a peculiar people zealous of good works.* Moreover, as if these motives were not sufficient, he every where makes the practice of moral duties an absolute condition of salvation. ʷ *The wrath of God is revealed against all ungodliness and unrighteousness.* ˣ *Because of these things cometh the wrath of God upon the children of disobedience.* ʸ *The unrighteous shall not inherit the kingdom of God.* ᶻ *Fol-*

---

a matter of such mean consequence; and set forth the wonderful love of God in the great work of our redemption merely to infer from it, that men ought to be careful to employ themselves in some honest trade or calling? As to *Grotius*'s interpretation of καλῶν ἔργων προΐστασθχ præesse bonis *operibus*— it is surely more agreeable to the context, more worthy of apostolical advice, and more honourable for Christians, that they should be patterns and precedents of holiness, the chief and foremost, eminent and remarkable above all others in the discharge of moral and religious duties, than that they should be examples of diligence and industry, presiding and looking over their families in the exercise of a trade however honest and useful.

ʷ *Rom.* i, 18.   ˣ *Ephes.* v. 6.
ʸ 1 *Cor.* vi. 9.   ᶻ *Heb.* xii. 14.

low

low holiness, without which no man shall see the Lord.

Upon the whole then St. *Paul* evidently concurs with the other apostles in carrying on with the greatest uniformity the cause of evangelical righteousness, to which alone our Saviour has annexed the reward of eternal happiness. This righteousness (as has, I flatter myself, been abundantly proved) consists in *faith in Christ and obedience to his commands*. These will through the grace of God and the satisfaction of *Christ* assuredly and effectually procure our justification and salvation: through the *grace of God* I say, as the *principal efficient* cause by which fallen man is restored to his favour; through the *satisfaction of Christ*, as the *meritorious* cause for the sake of which God pardons, justifies, and bestows eternal life upon those who sincerely perform the conditions of *faith* and *obedience* required in the evangelical covenant.

It ill becomes us to pry too curiously into and dogmatically pronounce upon

God's secret decrees: but it is every man's bounden duty, written in plain characters upon the mind of every man, to obey with awe and reverence his express commands. Scripture cannot be at variance with itself. We ought therefore so to temper the sense of passages seemingly contradictory, as to rob neither of that honour and submission which is due to every part of the word of God. When therefore salvation is ascribed to his *free grace*, we ought to conclude that *our own endeavours* are supposed to co-operate with it: when we are exhorted to *work* out our own salvation, we ought not to exclude the concurrence of his *grace*, by which [a] *his strength is made perfect in our weakness*. When we are said to be justified through *faith*, we should understand such a faith as is productive of *good works:* when we read of the glorious promises made to *good works*, we must confine them to such works only as spring from a true lively *faith* in *Jesus Christ*.

[b] *What therefore God hath joined together, let not man put asunder*. Let us not so abuse

[a] 2 Cor. xii. 9.   [b] Matth. xix. 6.

the

the *mercy* of God as to refuse him our *obedience:* let us not think so highly of our obedience as to depreciate his mercy. Let us ^c *acknowledge the truth which is after godliness*; so entirely depend upon the grace of God and the merits of our Saviour, as if our own endeavours were altogether insignificant and useless; and be at the same time so active and laborious in the ways of righteousness and holiness, as if we were able by the strength and power of nature alone to ^d *work the works of God*, and ^e *lay hold on eternal life.* Finally therefore (to conclude with the words with which I began) *Finally, brethren, whatsoever things are true, whatsoever things are honest, whatsoever things are just, whatsoever things are pure, whatsoever things are lovely, whatsoever things are of good report; if there be any virtue, and if there be any praise, think on these things.*

^c *Tit.* i. 1.   ^d *John* vi. 28.
^e 1 *Tim.* vi. 12.

A Vindication of St. Paul *from the charge of wishing himself accursed:*

A

SERMON

PREACHED BEFORE THE

UNIVERSITY OF OXFORD.

Rom. ix. 2, 3.

I have great heaviness and continual sorrow in my heart. For I could wish that myself were accursed from Christ for my brethren.

[a] THERE is something so exceedingly unnatural in the wish supposed to be contained in this portion of scripture, that notwithstanding all the pains taken by learned and pious men to explain and qualify it, I cannot be induced to think that it ever proceeded from the great Apostle to whom it is attributed. The very subject he is treating of seems to me a most evi-

---

[a] If any person is desirous of knowing the different modes of explaining and qualifying this passage hitherto attempted, let him consult *Witsius*'s Dissertation upon it in the 2d volume of his *Miscellanea Sacra*.

dent and absolute demonstration to the contrary. In the preceding chapter he sets forth the glorious privileges of God's elect: it begins with a triumphant declaration that [b] *there is no condemnation to them that are in Christ Jesus,* and ends in the same exulting strain, with a firm persuasion [c] *that neither death, nor life, nor angels, nor principalities, nor powers, nor things present, nor things to come, nor height, nor depth, nor any other creature, shall be able to separate us from the love of God which is in Christ Jesus our Lord.* Can it be imagined that he would in the very next sentence wish to be cut off from that salvation on which he dwells with such rapturous ardency of expression? Could he, who was taught Christianity by *Christ* himself, conceive that his own damnation could in any wise contribute to the glory of God or the happiness of his brethren? Such a supposition surely is absurd and impious: and however the words are modified into a figurative hyperbolical expression, denoting the fervency of his zeal and affection;

[b] C. viii. 1.   [c] V. 38, 39.

how-

however qualified into an hypothetical or conditional enuntiation, fignifying only that were it poffible or proper he *could wifh to be accurfed from Chrift*; they ftill feem to contain in them matter at which human nature fhudders, againft which right reafon and Chriftianity revolt.

To refcue the Apoftle from the imputation of fo extravagant a declaration is my defign in the following difcourfe: in order to which I fhall endeavour to prove that his words have in reality a very different meaning; and confirm the expofition which I fhall give of them by fhewing (from a few obfervations on the character of the *Jews*, that of St. *Paul*, and the *doctrines* here treated of) that it tends to illuftrate the whole tenour of the Apoftle's argument, and the peculiar manner in which he enforces it upon the prepoffeffions and prejudices of thofe whom he addreffes.

'The paffage, as it now ftands, is in-

[d] St. *Paul*, as his manner is (fays father *Simon*) expreffes himfelf in fo few words, that we muft fupply fomething to fhew the caufe of his great forrow; which the words that follow feem to point at.

con-

conclusive: it declares the Apostle's great uneasiness and sorrow; but makes no mention of the cause or object of it. This may be remedied by uniting the two verses into one period, and throwing that part of it which we render *I could wish that myself were accursed from Christ* into a parenthesis: for then the context will be full and explicit—*I have great heaviness and continual sorrow in my heart for, or on account of my brethren.* The sentence, which I dismember as it were from the rest, runs thus in the original ηὐχόμην γὰρ αὐτὸς ἐγὼ εἶναι ἀνάθεμα ἀπὸ τοῦ χριστοῦ. The word ηὐχόμην does not seem to me to be *potential*, but barely to denote something which the Apostle had formerly done; neither do I conceive the least idea of a wish annexed to it in this place. It does undoubtedly often signify *to wish* or *pray for:* [e] it moreover signifies

---

[e] εὔχεαι, λέγεις—εὔχεαι, λέγειν—εὐχόμεθα, φαμέν. *Hesych.* σημαίνει δὲ τὸ κυρίως λέγειν ᾗ ἁπλῶς. ἀγχιάλοιο διίφρονος ηὔχομαι εἶναι υἱός—εὔχετο δ' ἐξ Ἰθάκης ἔμμεναι. *Etym. Magn.* The Lexicons will supply many other instances. The word δοκεῖν seems to be of a somewhat similar nature. Thus οἱ δοκοῦντες ἄρχειν Mark x. 42. is the same as οἱ ἄρχοντες Matth. xx. 25.— and οἱ βασιλεῖς Luke xxii. 25. Thus in our Apostle's *first Ep. to the Cor.* vii. 40. δοκῶ πνεῦμα θεοῦ ἔχειν signifies *I have the spirit of God.* ὁ δοκῶν ἑστάναι, x. 12. *he that*

to *profess*, and is likewise very frequently *pleonastical*. One single sentence which occurs in almost every page of *Homer* will fully explain my meaning. That poet usually observes, upon the introduction of a distinguished hero, that διὸς παῖς ηὐχετο εἶναι i. e. *He gloried in being*, or *he professed that he was*, or simply *he was the son of Jupiter.* St. *Paul*'s phraseology is exactly the same; and therefore I conclude that in the same plain, natural, and obvious sense of the word he here declares that *he himself once gloried in being, he himself once professed that he was*, or simply *he himself once was* ἀνάθεμα ἀπὸ τοῦ χριστοῦ : for the words αὐτὸς ἐγω ought undoubtedly in the construction immediately to precede ηὐχόμην, not εἶναι, as in our translation; they seem moreover to imply that whatever was the Apostle's object was also the object of those whom he addresses, αὐτὸς ἐγω *I myself likewise as well as you.* This object was ἀνάθεμα εἶναι ἀπὸ τοῦ Χριστοῦ; which words, according to the [f] authorities cited by Dr. *Whitby* from the

---

that stands. ὁ δοκῶν εἶναι φιλόνεικος xi. 16. *he that is contentious*—εἴ τις δοκεῖ προφήτης εἶναι, xiv. 37. *if any man be a prophet.*

[f] Orig. Chrysost. Theod. Oec. Phot. Theophyl.

Greek

Greek fathers, are of the same import as ἀλλότριον εἶναι τοῦ Χριστοῦ, χωρισθῆναι τῆς ἀγάπης, ἐκπεσεῖν τῆς δόξης *to be an alien from Christ, to be separated from his love, to fall from the glory and salvation purchased by him.*

The Apostle is generally, and I think justly, supposed to have the Jewish excommunications in view, and particularly that kind of them called *Cherem*, usually expressed in *Greek* by the word ἀνάθεμα; in which to the deprivation of the commerce and benefits of society were added curses and execrations, and the person upon whom this punishment was inflicted [g] *was utterly detested and utterly abhorred, for he was a cursed thing.* To this the Apostle alludes, to show the wretchedness of *his former* and by implication *their present* situation. *I myself*, says he, *likewise once was an accursed thing, an alien from Christ, cut off from his love, and excommunicated from all share in the glory and salvation purchased by him.* And to what state more properly, than that wherein offen-

[g] *Deut.* vii. 26.

ders among themselves were stripped of all the honours and blessings attending a member of the visible church — to what state, I say, could he more properly compare the rejection of the *Jews*, and their exclusion from the peculiar covenant of God? This was the doctrine he was then entering upon: he had been preparing them for it by laying before them with all the display of language the law's inability to save, the satisfaction of *Christ*, and the inestimable value of all the evangelical privileges—Yet he does not even then begin so offensive a subject abruptly; he first of all endeavours to engage their attention, and bespeak their good will by a [h] solemn asseveration of his sincerity, and an affectionate allusion to their own kind and tender behaviour towards those whom they looked upon as lost and dead unto God.

---

[h] St. *Paul's* frequent protestations of his affection to the *Jews* seem strongly to intimate that he was suspected of being an enemy to his own nation, on account of the doctrines which he preached—*viz.* the exclusion of the *Jews*, and the admission of the *Gentiles*—That this was really the case we are told by several of the Fathers—See in particular *Irenæus* l. 1. c. 26. and *Euseb. Hist. Eccles.* l. 3. c. 27.

¹ For it was a custom among the *Jews* to put on solemn mourning, to fast and humble themselves, and by every mark of sorrow shew their sympathy with a person laid under a *cherem* or *anathema*, bewailing him as one who was dead. To this custom I apprehend the Apostle to refer — *I say the truth in Christ, I lie not, my conscience also bearing me witness in the Holy Ghost that I have great heaviness and continual sorrow in my heart.* Thus cautiously does he proceed before he ventures to declare truths which he knows must be displeasing and ungrateful: and yet he here again stops short. He was going to declare the reason of his sorrow — *viz.* their being cut off from all share in the salvation purchased by the *Messiah*, their being excommunicated from *Christ* as he himself

---

¹ This custom likewise obtained in the Christian church. μῇ λύπης ᾗ πένθης ἀνιάτως ἔχοντα τῆς ἐκκλησίας ἀποκόπτε *cut off from the church a person that is incurable with sorrow and mourning* is one of the *apostolical constitutions*. l. 2. 41. To this custom St. *Paul* seems to allude, 1 *Cor.* v. 2. — 2 *Cor.* ii. 1. 3. and xii. 21. From the *Jews Pythagoras* in all probability borrowed the custom mentioned by *Jamblicus* in his life, c. 17. by *Clem. Alex. Strom.* 5. and by *Origen* p. 67 — 142. of putting up cenotaphs in his school in the room of those who had deserted it.

once

once was: yet he here again stops short, and by an elegant transition turns for a moment the discourse from *them*, and names no offender but *himself*; yet in such a manner as by a strong though delicate insinuation to imply their being involved in the same misery: and when he does mention them as the object of his grief and affliction, he does it by the endearing title of *brethren* accompanied with a recital of the gracious respects with which they were favoured beyond any other nation under heaven. *I have great heaviness and continual sorrow in my heart (for I myself likewise once was an excommunicate outcast from Christ) on account of my brethren, my kinsmen according to the flesh: who are Israelites; to whom pertaineth the adoption, and the glory, and the covenants, and the giving of the law; and the service of God, and the promises; whose are the fathers, and of whom as concerning the flesh Christ came; who is over all God blessed for ever. Amen.*

^k There is in the history of the *Jews*

---

^k See *Cunæus de Rep. Heb.* l. 2. c. 17.

among many others this one very remarkable circumstance; that whereas before the Babylonish captivity there were no ecclesiastical schisms but frequent apostacies, on the contrary after that period we read of no apostacies, but numberless schisms, various and dangerous heresies. While the spirit of prophecy dwelled among them, and God could be on all occasions consulted, there was no room for disputes or controversies; God must either be implicitly obeyed, or totally renounced. But when his more immediate interposition was withdrawn, and the church committed to the care of a standing ministry; prophetical and oracular declarations of his will (those great glories of the first temple) were succeeded by the precarious comments of their doctors, revelation by opinion. Hence arose various sects, each of which with a partiality too common to human nature cherished their own offspring; listened with more complacency, and adhered with more zeal to the suggestions of their own fancy, than they had ever done to the oracles of those infallible guides, whom God had set over them. Yet the remembrance
of

of the grievous calamities they had suffered so effectually wrought upon them, that there appeared under the second temple no traces of that proneness to idolatry, which had brought down the severest of God's judgements upon their church and nation. Add to this that the different sects having, or pretending to have, the law for their basis, every one of them however differing in all other points agreed notwithstanding in this, *viz.* that every part of it whether moral, judicial, or ceremonial, was of eternal and immutable obligation; and we must do them the justice to acknowledge, that in [1] many instances they bore with heroic firmness the cruellest persecutions rather than depart from the least tittle of it. This law their forefathers had received from the hand of God himself; with them he had made a covenant, and had adopted the whole nation; where-

---

[1] Particularly under *Ptolomy Philopater*; when out of many thousand *Jews*, which dwelt at *Alexandria*, only three hundred forsook their God to gain the favour of the king. The rest, though at the danger of their lives, stood all firm to the religion of their forefathers, and expressed the utmost abhorrence at the apostacy of their brethren. See *Prideaux*'s *Connection*, part 2. book 2.

by they became his [m] *peculiar people,* his [n] *first born,* the [o] *heirs of the promises.* Entrenched within thefe glorious privileges they thought themfelves fecure, whilft they maintained the outworks of ritual obfervances; and adhering to the rigour of the letter looked upon the favour of God as their own peculiar and indefeafible inheritance, fondly appropriating to themfelves exclufively of all other nations the promifed bleffings. But now the [p] *partition wall* was *broken down,* falvation preached to the Gentiles, and every one who profeffed faith in *Chrift* equally admitted into the covenant of grace. To explain this important point St. *Paul* enters largely into the true nature of the Jewifh oeconomy and of the covenant made with *Abraham;* proving to them by the ftrongeft arguments that it was not made in confequence of the law or of circumcifion; and that, as all the natural defcendants of *Abraham* were not comprehended in the promife, fo neither was it limited to *them* only; but that all, of whomfoever defcend-

[m] *Deut.* xiv. 2. [n] *Exod.* iv. 22.
[o] *Heb.* vi. 17. [p] *Ephef.* ii. 14.

ed,

ed, who followed the steps of the father of the faithful, were *that spiritual* seed to whom the promise was made. The admission therefore of the believing *Gentiles* into the kingdom of the *Messiah* was a fulfilling of the promise, every title to which the *Jews* had forfeited by their infidelity, and rendered themselves incapable of the blessings by refusing the terms of acceptance and salvation which God himself had proposed.

So harsh and unpleasing a doctrine required great skill and management. We have already observed how cautiously the Apostle introduces it; he employs the same tenderness and address throughout, with such arguments as refute their extravagant claims mixing such topics, as in some degree flattered their pride and prepossession. He allows and magnifies their high prerogatives and advantages; and, whilst he urges the stability of God's promises, he raises their hopes and expectations, by shewing that their rejection was neither total nor final, but that he had according to his free and gracious purpose reserved

reserved a remnant, and would in his own good time restore the whole nation to the glorious title of the *people of God*. That this comfortable assurance might leave the stronger impression upon their minds, and induce them to fulfil the counsel of God's goodness by their obedience, he closes with it the argumentative part of his discourse: but he does not entirely reserve it for that period; he touches upon it in the words which I have submitted to your consideration, uniting himself, to press his argument the stronger, familiarly with them—*I myself likewise was once an excommunicate outcast from Christ*—wherein he not only applies his former situation to their present case, but likewise represents to them by his example the method and assurance of recovering God's favour.

And what more forcible example could he set before them? who could with more propriety attack their prejudices than he, who was known to have ⁹ imbibed those

---

⁹ With these particulars (and he appeals to the *Jews* for the truth of them) St. *Paul* begins his defence before *Agrippa Acts* xxvi; that having thus previously secured the attention and prepossession of his hearers he might
urge

prejudices from his infancy; who had been educated and brought up in the strictest sect among them, had been remarkable for his more exceeding zeal for their religion and the bitterest enmity against Christianity? Who could with more energy and conviction lay before them the ʳ *exceeding riches of God's grace*, than he who to a more immediate and extraordinary operation of *that* grace owed his conversion and call to the apostleship? It is indeed a theme which he so particularly delights in, that one of the fathers has not scrupled to call him the *angel* or *messenger* of grace.

It is remarked of St. *John* the beloved disciple of *Christ*, that he seems to be inspired with a more generous affection, a

---

urge, with more confidence of gaining credit, the extraordinary manner in which he was converted. He had used the same address before in his defence to the *Jews* at *Jerusalem*, c. 22. *I am a Jew, brought up at the feet of Gamaliel, and taught according to the perfect manner of the law of the fathers, and was zealous towards God, and I persecuted this way unto the death, as also the high priest doth bear me witness, and all the estate of the elders, from whom I received letters and went to Damascus; and it came to pass*, &c.

ʳ *Ephes.* ii. 7.

more

more fervent *charity*, than the rest of the Apostles: full of that divine principle, by which he had been peculiarly distinguished, he urges it through all his epistles as the primary and essential law of Christianity; his discourses speak nothing, breathe nothing but love and *charity*. In like manner our Apostle, who had felt such powerful effects of God's *grace*, by which he had in a moment from a blasphemer been transformed into a saint, from a persecutor into a pastor, from an instrument of vengeance and death into a herald of peace and life — Our Apostle, I say (as if every faculty of his soul was entirely possessed by that glorious attribute from whose astonishing and more special influence he derived his spiritual being) takes every where occasion to extol and magnify the riches and the treasures of *grace*; he dwells upon it in this discourse with all the rapture of holy gratitude, till lost in the unfathomable ocean of God's counsels, by which his severest judgements conclude at last in mercy, he breaks out in *that* extatic exclamation which closes the whole argument

ment—'*O the depth of the riches both of the wisdom and the knowledge of God!* &c.

From the warmth of St. *Paul*'s temper some learned men have been led into a supposition that ᵗ he was prefigured by the patriarch *Jacob* in his prophecy concerning *Benjamin,* to whose tribe the Apostle belonged. ᵘ *Benjamin shall ravin as a wolf; in the morning he shall devour the prey, and at night he shall divide the spoil.*

I own I cannot discover the propriety of the application: I think with ʷ one of the brightest ornaments of our church that I see *better things* in the great Apostle of the Gentiles, ˣ *and things that accompany*

ˢ *Rom.* xi. 33.
ᵗ This was St. *Austin*'s opinion, as he tells us himself *in Nat. Mart. serm.* 333. *de Paulo Apost.* 279.
ᵘ *Genes.* xlix. 27. The fierce temper of this tribe, described under the character of a *wolf,* shewed itself on many occasions, especially in the war which it maintained against all the other tribes, *Judg.* xx. The latter part of the prophecy I take to have been verified in the equal right which that tribe had with *Judah* to the city of *Jerusalem,* its adherence with it to the line of *David,* and forming in conjunction with it, after the dispersion of the ten tribes, the whole nation of the *Jews.*
ʷ Mr. *Mede.*   ˣ *Heb.* vi. 9.

sal-

salvation. I cannot perſuade myſelf but I read repreſented in him the outlines of that myſterious diſpenſation which we are conſidering. His zeal for Judaiſm, his enmity againſt Chriſtianity, his miraculous and ſudden converſion, the extraordinary gifts and ſpecial revelations vouchſafed to him in conſequence of it, his being appointed the chief inſtrument in the hand of God for the converſion of the Gentiles are, if not emblems of, at leaſt very applicable to God's dealings with the whole Jewiſh nation.

[y] Among the various methods by which God was pleaſed to inſtruct his people under the law, he often made uſe of that of *ſimilitude*; the prophet aſſuming different emblematical characters, which they applying to themſelves might be made ſenſible of their condition and God's impending judgements. Thus [z] *Jeremiah* and

---

[y] *I have ſpoken by the prophets; and I have multiplied viſions; and uſed ſimilitudes by the miniſtry of the prophets.* Hoſ. xii. 10. See *Biſhop Chandler's Defence of Chriſtianity,* ch. 3. ſect. 1.

[z] *Jerem.* xiii. 27. 32.

ᵃ *Ezekiel* are upon several occasions *a sign unto them*; they presignify and represent by their actions what God had commanded them to declare of his counsels and designs. ᵇ *Hosea*'s wife and children were patterns and figures of the idolatry, desolation, and restoration of *Israel*. ᶜ *Behold* (saith *Isaiah*) *I and the children whom the Lord hath given me are for signs and wonders,* i. e. types and symbols, *in Israel from the Lord of hosts.* Why may we not be allowed to suppose that God might, under the second covenant, condescend to convey instruction in a manner familiarized to them by the frequent ministry of his prophets, and raise from among them an exemplar of his dealings with them, a visible pledge of his promises, a remembrancer of his veracity and their duty? Might not at least the Apostle, ᵈ eminently skilled as he was in their ab-

---

ᵃ *Ezech* iv. 12. 24.   ᵇ See *Hos.* c. i. throughout.
ᶜ *If.* viii. 18.

ᵈ *It is plain to him that hath carefully read St. Paul's Epistles, and is acquainted also with the writings of Philo, that the holy Apostle well understood the cabalistical theology of the Jews.* Bull's Sermon on 2 *Tim.* iv. 13. Father *Simon* says that a *Jew,* well versed in ancient cabalistical authors, freely owned to him that the *Epistle to the Hebrews* must have been written by some great *Mekubal* or *master of tradition.* Far from charging St. *Paul* with having perverted
the

ſtruſer learning, make uſe of the *ſymbolical*
method of argumentation in which they ſo
much delighted to work upon their affections; and temper the ſeverity of his
doctrine by prefiguring to them under his
own character, that though they were then
*aliens, outcaſts, excommunicated, anathema-
tized from Chriſt,* yet ſhould they again be
admitted into the pale of his church, the
ſociety and privileges of the faithful? Sure
I am that he ſtrongly inſiſts upon this ex-
emplification in the beginning of the *eleventh* chapter. *Hath God caſt away his
people? God forbid: for I alſo am an Iſrae-
lite, of the ſeed of Abraham, of the tribe of
Benjamin. God hath not caſt away his people
whom he foreknew. Wot ye not what the
ſcripture ſaith of Elias, how he maketh inter-
ceſſion to God againſt Iſrael? ſaying, Lord
they have killed thy prophets and digged down
thy altars, and I am left alone, and they ſeek
my life. But what ſaith the anſwer of God
to him? I have reſerved to myſelf ſeven thou-*

---

the true ſenſe of ſcripture by his allegories, he highly commended his deep knowledge of the ſublime meaning of the
Bible, and was always full of his great *Mekubal,* of whom
he never ſpoke but with admiration. *Hiſt. Crit. du* N. T.
p. 248.

ſand

sand men, who have not bowed the knee to the image of Baal. Even so then at this present time also there is a remnant according to the election of grace. As the Apostle here confessedly instances *Elias* and the seven thousand faithful amidst a former general defection of the *Jews*, as a proof that God had not absolutely and without exception rejected his people; so likewise does he by parity of reason instance himself, hold himself forth as a type, as a pledge and earnest of their future restoration, notwithstanding their present national infidelity, to the glorious blessings promised to their forefathers; when like him they exchange external federation for inward obedience, and accept the covenant of grace by faith in *Jesus Christ. For*, as he declares himself to his favourite disciple *Timothy*, [e] *for this cause he obtained mercy, that in him first Jesus Christ might shew forth all long-suffering for a pattern to them which should hereafter believe on him to eternal life.*

That there will be hereafter a general conversion of the *Jews* to the Christian faith

[e] 1 *Tim.* i. 16.

faith cannot, I think, be doubted by any one who reads with the least degree of attention the prophecies of the Old and New Testament, and particularly what St. *Paul* (who was in a more especial manner intrusted with this mystery) plainly and professedly declares concerning it in the *eleventh* chapter of this epistle. In what manner God will be pleased to bring about this gracious dispensation is in no part of scripture expressly revealed; but from the importance of the event we may conclude that the means used will be more than ordinary: and this conclusion is confirmed by those passages of holy writ which the consentient opinion of learned and pious men apply to this transaction. They plainly indicate some special manifestation of God, always representing *Christ* as ʃ *appear-*

ʃ We are told by St. *Luke* in the first chapter of the *Acts* that *while the apostles beheld, our Saviour was taken up and a cloud received him out of their sight. And—behold two men stood by them in white apparel, which also said—this same Jesus which is taken up from you into heaven* shall so come in like manner as ye have seen him go into heaven. Our Saviour himself tells us—*Then shall appear the sign of the son of man in heaven; and then shall all the tribes of the earth mourn*—(compare *Rev.* i. 7. and *Zechar.* xii. 10.) *and they shall see the son of man* coming in the clouds of heaven with power

ing in the clouds (that constant symbol of the divine presence) *with power and great glory.* Our Saviour's similar revelation of himself to St. *Paul* and the effects wrought by it were unexpected and instantaneous; and we have reason to conclude that the conversion of the whole nation of the *Jews* will in like manner be as sudden and surprising as the outward means used to effect it are extraordinary and miraculous. ^g *I will remove the iniquity of that land in one day,* saith God by the mouth of his prophet *Zechariah*—This is beautifully and emphatically expressed by the evangelical prophet. ^h *Before she travailed she brought forth; before her pain came, she was delivered of a man child. Who hath heard such a thing? who hath seen such things? shall the earth be made to bring forth in one day? or shall a nation be born at once? for as soon as Zion travailed, she brought forth her children.* Then will God's promises of spiritual blessings be fulfilled: ⁱ *God will*

---

power and great glory. *Matth* xxiv. 30. See *Mark* xiii. 26. *Luke* xxi. 27. *John* xiv. 3. *Dan.* vii. 13. &c.
^g *Zechar.* iii. 9. ^h *If.* lxvi. 7, 8.
ⁱ *If.* xl. 3. liv. 13.

pour

pour his spirit upon their seed, and his blessing upon their offspring. All their children shall be taught of God. There is surely a more than casual coincidence between this last circumstance and the extraordinary manner in which St. *Paul* received his doctrine: he was literally *taught of God.* [k] *Paul an apostle not of men, neither by man, but by Jesus Christ and God the father.* As he received his commission, so did he likewise his instructions without the intervention of any human instrument immediately and entirely from *Christ* himself. [l] *I certifie you, brethren, that the gospel which was preached of me is not after man; for I neither received it of man, neither was I taught it but by the revelation of Jesus Christ.* No wonder that he who was so highly favoured should be more learned than the rest of the apostles in the mystical truths of Christianity — (They were part of the [m] *unspeakable words* which *he heard when he was caught up into paradise*) — and more particularly the treasures of God's mercy to the heathen world, which he

---

[k] *Galat.* i. 1.
[m] 2 *Cor.* xii. 4.
[l] *Galat.* i. 14, 12.

was

was in a more efpecial manner commiffioned to promulgate. "*By revelation he made known unto me the myftery—that the Gentiles fhould be fellow-heirs and of the fame body and partakers of his promife in Chrift by the gofpel, whereof I was made a minifter according to the gift of the grace of God given unto me by the effectual working of his power.* By which laft words I underftand the wonderful fuccefs and efficacy which attended his miniftry among the Gentiles, on which account he applies to himfelf that prophecy of *Ifaiah*: °*To whom he was not spoken of they fhall fee, and they that have not heard fhall underftand.* This fuccefs, great as it was, was but a faint glimmering of that marvellous light; which, while it ᵖ *lightens the Gentiles,* fhall be *the glory of* God's *people Ifrael*. As the Apoftle was to the *Jews* a pledge of their future ᑫ releafe from the ἀνάθεμα they then laboured under, fo were his *Gentile* converts the firft fruits of that glorious harveft, when the *fon of*

ⁿ *Ephef.* iii. 3. 6, 7.   ° *If.* lii. 15. *Rom.* xv. 21.
ᵖ *Luke* xii. 32.
ᑫ I cannot but think this to be the meaning of that paffage in the *Revelations*, κ᷽ πᾶν κατανάθεμα οὐκ ἔσαι ἔτι, c. xxii. 3.

Y   *man*

man shall thrust his sickle on the earth and the earth be reaped. They were an earnest that salvation shall be hereafter universally derived to them from *Israel*, when ' *out of Sion shall* once more *go forth the law, and the word of the Lord from Jerusalem.* For ' *if the fall of them be the riches of the world, and the diminishing of them the riches of the Gentiles; how much more their fulness? And if the casting away of them be the reconciling of the world, what shall the receiving of them be but life from the dead?*

These mysteries *angels* themselves ' *desire to look into:* they are not vain speculations, but venerable truths; from which (would time permit) many sublime and important conclusions might be deduced. Even from the obstinacy of the Jews several arguments in favour of Christianity might be drawn; the authenticity of holy writ might fairly be inferred from that almost incredible care, which their pertinacious attachment to the law induced them to bestow upon the Scriptures; they not

r *Micah* iv. 2.   s *Rom.* xi. 12. 15.
t 1 Pet. i. 12.

only

only learned them from their childhood, but even reckoned every word, every syllable, every letter: those passages in particular which relate to the *Messiah* are a standing evidence against themselves, and being preserved and acknowledged as genuine by the avowed enemies of *Christ* cannot be disputed by any patrons of infidelity.

What a noble scheme of justice and mercy is displayed in God's dealings with his once favourite people? What a forcible lesson does their rejection read to us against spiritual pride, security, and presumption? What a comfortable argument do God's promises of taking them again into favour furnish us with against religious melancholy and despair?—The same and other ample matter of useful consideration is afforded us in St. *Paul*'s character both before and after his conversion. We have in his conversation painted in the strongest colours the deformity of prejudice, the odiousness of a blind ungovernable zeal, of a fierce persecuting spirit. But how beautifully are these contrasted by by a docile obedience to the evidence of truth, affection for his brethren, patience under sufferings and reproaches for the sake of *Christ*, unwearied diligence in preaching the gospel, constancy and perseverance in it even unto death?

These topics I might enlarge upon, would time permit, to our mutual satisfaction and improvement. And yet, if time *did* permit, I should be unwilling to draw off your attention from *that* glorious scene to which I have endeavoured to trace the mystery of u *the unsearchable riches of Christ*. This is that w *manifestation of the sons of God for which the earnest expectation of the creature waiteth*; that kingdom of God for which our Saviour has commanded us to pray; of whose amplitude there shall be no bound, of whose duration no end; in which x *righteousness shall dwell*, and y *the work of righteousness shall be peace, and the effect of righteousness quietness and assurance for ever*.

u *Ephes.* iii. 8.   w *Rom.* viii. 19.
x *2 Pet.* iii. 13.   y *Is.* xxxii. 17.

Let us therefore, *[z] who are delivered from the bondage of corruption into the glorious liberty of the children of God, [a] walk worthy of the vocation wherewith we are called, [b] in all holy conversation and godliness looking for and hastening the coming of the day of God*; beseeching him that he would shortly accomplish the number of his elect, have mercy upon all *aliens from Christ*, take from them all ignorance, hardness of heart and contempt of his word; and so bring them home to his flock, that they may be saved among the remnant of the true Israelites, and be made one fold under one shepherd *Jesus Christ* our Lord, who liveth and reigneth with the Father and the holy spirit, one God world without end. *Amen.*

[z] *Rom.* viii. 21.   [a] *Ephes.* iv. 1.
[b] *2 Pet.* iii. 12.

F I N I S.

www.ingramcontent.com/pod-product-compliance
Lightning Source LLC
Chambersburg PA
CBHW031432230426
43668CB00007B/501